wrotelio™

Malene Jorgensen – Data Lemonade: Achieving the Best Digital Marketing Results Using Data and Marketing Psychology

ISBN-Print: 978-1-77181-091-3
ISBN Hardcover: 978-1-77181-092-0
ISBN-E-Book: 978-1-77181-093-7
ISBN Audiobook: 978-1-77181-094-4

- Dedication -

For those thirsty for knowledge; may your brain always be steeped in curiosity and served with a twist of data.

- Table of Contents -

- Introduction -

"What's the expected ROI?"

If you've worked in marketing for more than 10 minutes, you've probably heard your boss or your client ask this exact question. "Ah, well, I mean - that's hard to predict here," you stutter, wondering how you are going to share that predicting an exact ROI is one of the *most* challenging parts of marketing.

Even *after* you've run a digital marketing campaign, explaining the exact ROI isn't easy, despite you having a mountain of data to sift through. Sure, there's the financial return on investment, which is direct revenue that correlates to the amount spent on the given campaign.

But there are many other factors that influence your *actual* return and some are not as easily measured as the financial numbers. Why? Well, how do you exactly measure the impact of your marketing?

I've been in digital marketing for close to two decades as I'm writing this book and if you have worked with me during those 20 years, I'd be surprised to hear if you haven't heard me compare digital marketing to dating. Yes, dating.

Here's the thing - just because you put a product or service into the world does not mean you get a return on your investment immediately that can easily be measured with a linear path to success. In fact, it rarely happens that way. Just like in dating - you don't go on a blind dinner date and walk out of the restaurant with a fiancé. I mean, sure - could that be the premise of a reality show? Probably. But that's far from the norm and I - for one - would be hesitant to plan my future based on a proposal happening on the first date. I'd probably go hide in the bathroom while booking an Uber and escape through the kitchen with the help of the restaurant staff.

If you've picked up this book, chances are you are ready to learn more about digital marketing data and discover how to turn a not-so-great data situation into one where you can leverage the power to scale profits, solutions and innovation.

And that is easier said than done, as data isn't always as sweet and straightforward as you'd like. It's often a sour lemon that has been neglected for far too long - yes, such as a data set with missing entries, fragmented information or simply completely outdated. Of course, there was a good intention somewhere that 'someday we'll do something about it.'

If you are sitting with a CRM, a social dashboard, an ad account, or an email platform packed with outdated data or old exported data sets, I'm here to tell you that the time is now to gather fresh data. It's not that your existing data is useless - but with the right tools, the right mindset and a strategic approach, you can transform your data into something incredibly valuable.

Everything we do is tied to data. You purchase something at the store - your products are tracked to ensure inventory is restocked so there's a supply for the next customer. You wear a smartwatch - your steps are tracked, your heart rate is stored, and all of the data feeds back into your device. You unlock your phone and engage with content - you are tracked by clicks, time, and engagement.

For digital marketers, performance data is everywhere. From website clicks to consumer behaviour on social media, everything you do is tracked and can be used to improve performance. Every single transaction done in the online world leaves a trail of valuable marketing data that can be used to optimize performance, scale solutions and be the seed behind innovative thinking.

And yet, performance data can be incredibly difficult and overwhelming when presented in a spreadsheet with figures that are well - just figures. Impressions, clicks, conversions - what does it all mean if not supported by a strong contextual base?

The goal with *Data Lemonade* is to help you make sense of marketing data and teach you some of the principles that surface in digital marketing that are tied directly to marketing psychology and trust-building practices. The thing is - sometimes, the notion of trust is a much more valuable ROI than the financial number on a report. But trust is not a measurable metric and prospect and consumer behaviours, along with qualitative data, can help you make sense of how your business or solution is positioned in the market.

Throughout this book, I'll share what core metrics every marketer should know, what marketing psychology tactics you should practice, and how you can leverage data to tell an analytical story rather than just presenting metrics to your clients. I wrote this book to hammer home a single point - and that is - the world of marketing is ever-evolving. That includes the addition of AI in recent years. Understanding data is no longer optional. Throwing spaghetti at the wall to see what sticks is no longer a possibility. You have to make data-driven decisions to see success and in order to do so, you need clean data to work with. If you can analyze data, speak to the metrics and share the story that it tells, you'll be successful in digital marketing. Data is at the heart of everything from content strategy to advertising, email marketing to full-scale ABM campaigns, and proactive thinking for innovative products or services.

By the end of this book, you'll be well-equipped to harness the power of digital marketing data, blend it with psychology and drive meaningful results. How? Because data tells a story - good or bad. Data is your compass and you can help shape the journey you want to take. By understanding that human behaviour in digital marketing is rarely ever linear, you can uncover potential patterns, bottlenecks and opportunities that can influence your marketing and sales efforts.

So, let's grab the virtual lemon squeezer and let's make some lemonade.

- Chapter 1 -

What is Data Lemonade?

The name for this book was inspired by the metaphorical expression of "turning lemons into lemonade" - to make the best of a bad situation or find a positive outcome from something unpleasant. Only a few people enjoy eating lemons as a fruit, including my own mom - which is something I will never understand, but like most people, I prefer lemonade. Turning something I don't enjoy into something I do.

I've worked in digital marketing since 2009, a year after the Global Financial Crisis that caused a major economic downturn, leading to the Great Recession. Back then, the digital landscape looked vastly different. We did not have access to all of the digital data we do now. Heck, Instagram wasn't even really around back then and Facebook was slowly becoming a common platform to connect with friends and upload every single event to share with the world.

With the surge of online platforms came more sign-ups. And with this, more personal data. These platforms became more complex, using user data to build out new features to get more engagement. And thus, more user data. In other words, with more data, the more these platforms were able to understand what people were doing on the platforms, what resulted in engagement, what kept people on the platform for longer, and subsequently, how to get ads in front of users that resulted in high conversion rates.

All of this was done using data; collecting data, analyzing the data and pivoting on the opportunities that the data revealed. The social platforms were not built by putting all the eggs in a single basket and hoping it would work out.

You may remember the poking feature on Facebook, where people could send pokes to one another. You may still find that feature if you look hard enough. Or the "nearby friends" feature that allowed you to find your friends nearby based on your physical location. Facebook also tested virtual gifts for two years back in 2008, allowing you to pay money to send virtual gifts to people, such as a picture of a chocolate box. Yup, that was a thing. Or what about the Facebook Beacon - a feature that would broadcast where people were buying online directly onto the Facebook feed, causing an uproar because it supposedly ruined Christmas back in the late 2000s.

Some of these features would probably be illegal now, given how privacy laws have changed over the years to protect users and consumers. But the point is - Facebook evolved because they gathered and analyzed the data that users provided them through their engagements and behaviours and pivoted.

The same kind of strategic methods can be used in digital marketing; gather the data, analyze the data, and pivot based on what it tells you and align that with your goal.

Every click, interaction, and engagement is a data point waiting to be interpreted and used. But how can you - as a marketer - ensure you're using this data effectively? Well, that's where Data Lemonade comes in - the idea that, just like turning sour lemons into refreshing lemonade, data can be transformed into actionable insights that power marketing strategies.

This metaphor not only provides a fun way to think about data - especially if you are looking at data that's significantly below industry benchmarks - but also highlights the importance of data literacy.

Whether you're looking at social media performance data, paid media campaigns data or email engagement rates, these figures are just raw data figures. The challenge comes when trying to interpret the numbers in a broader sense. What are they truly telling you in a contextual sense? What actions, thoughts, beliefs, motives, desires and decisions come through these numbers?

Turning those numbers into useful information requires a combination of analytical thinking and a solid understanding of marketing psychology - that whole, turning lemons into lemonade idea. Or in a more creative voice, turning the sourness of raw data into the sweet success of marketing campaigns that provide an actual return on investment.

Now, if you're thinking, "Great, I'm not Mark Zuckerberg and I don't have the creative thinking or the coding background to start a social platform" - fear not. It's not too late to discover opportunities through data.

You don't need to build a social platform to get data. Zuckerberg didn't start Facebook with the mission to become one of the richest people in the world. In fact, his early vision for Facebook was to create a platform that connected people at Harvard University, where he himself was a student. He wanted to make an impact on people without money being his priority - funny enough. And if he kept the user base to Harvard, there's a chance he wouldn't have discovered the power of data.

One of the most popular streaming services, Netflix, launched in 1997. At the time, co-founder Reed Hastings was growing frustrated with the late fees from Blockbuster. Those $40 late fees ruined the fun and his idea of creating a subscription service was ignited.

Remember Blockbuster? You'd hit up movie rental store on the weekends, walk the aisles to find the next movie you wanted to bring home - with the caveat that you had to bring it back within 48 hours for the next person waiting to watch it - or face that hefty late fee.

The newest movies were almost always on a waitlist. And the late fees killed the fun of bringing the movies home. Marc Randolph, the other half of Netflix's success, wanted to create an online experience, mirroring Amazon's online marketplace success.

While Hastings reportedly always had the vision that Netflix would become a streaming service, it wasn't until 2007 - 10 years after the initial launch - that the company went all-in on the streaming service. And how do you ensure that people continue to hand over their hard-earned money each and every month? You focus on subscribers' needs.

You need to keep them glued to the screen. They had a bowl full of lemons and chose to make lemonade by using subscribers' engagement data to keep them hooked. Netflix's recommendation system - you know, the one that puts a similar flick on the screen after you've successfully finished a movie or a show - utilizes data analytics to personalize your experience.

Netflix isn't just tracking what you are watching in terms of genres. They are also tracking how much you watch, your viewing history on the platform, how you rate shows and movies, and even the time of day you watch certain things. Netflix also tracks what you search for, and your social data, such as what your friends are watching to encourage recommendations that you'll actually love.

They don't just focus on one data set. They gather lots of different data points based on their users, and layer that with machine learning algorithms, including similar viewing habits, content metadata describers, deep learning to predict future preferences, and non-static search and home pages.

In short - lots of clean first-party data to deliver the best possible results for their viewers to encourage more viewer engagement.

Another example that you may frequently be taking advantage of is Amazon's Personalized Shopping

Experience. Amazon leverages customer data to provide personalized product recommendations, tailored search results and targeted marketing campaigns. Ever wonder how Amazon always puts the right products in front of you, saving you time and effort so you don't have to go find them yourself? Well, it's all data-driven personalization, resulting in greater sales built on automation. This personalized data strategy results in an enhanced shopping experience, increased sales and customer loyalty - all because the shopper feels seen, heard, and understood.

There are a few takeaways I want you to remember here as we get started on this larger data journey together. Firstly, you don't have to plan a blueprint for data collection out of the gate. Zuckerberg didn't plan on Facebook to be one of the most powerful companies in the world based on the amount of data it has on its users. That came over time. Instead, be open to the data you collect from people and keep it organized. A pattern or opportunity may reveal itself as you continue to try new things.

Secondly, focus on gathering as much data as possible. If you look at a general contact form on a website, it's often your default fields; name, email, phone and message. Simple. Enough to get in touch with the prospects.

While "form friction" is real and conversions can suffer if you add too many fields - we're not doing a health intake form here - you can add a few additional fields to learn more about your prospects. For example, divide up the name into two fields, so you get first name and last name. A simple fix for easy personalization. Second, ask for interest or vertical if your business has defined verticals. Third, ask for a job title so you can track who is the initial point of contact - great, if you are dealing with multiple decision makers. Other options could be location, solutions interested in, or asking them to identify themselves as a persona you have built as your ICP. I'll return to the importance of form logic in a later chapter, so put a pin in that idea for now.

Thirdly, keep your data as clean as possible. In other words, keep it up to date, keep it in the right fields - so don't put email in a phone number field, or add multiple emails in a singular email field, keep your performance data on ads and social posts with dates and content context, and always ensure to keep your email lists clean of bounces, and spam.

Clean data helps you understand the bigger picture more efficiently, and it is easier to spot patterns that are useful and accurate.

And lastly, wait to draw any conclusions from your data until you have a large data set to work with. This may take months, as the data set may change based on seasonality, testing, campaigns and more. It's important to compare apples to apples rather than apples to oranges - or grapes, or berries. You get the drift.

Bad data can lead to bad strategies, generic outcomes, and a total brand misalignment. For example, let's say you watch horror movies 90% of the time, and you just watched a single rom-com flick because your significant other won control of the remote for a single night. If Netflix was going to make a decision on a single piece of data, then you probably wouldn't be happy with the outcome. Imagine logging in the next day, only seeing rom-com recommendations. Yikes.

The importance of data literacy is crucial to understand how your marketing efforts are doing, how your business is doing, and identifying areas where scalability is ideal. Understanding how to read data leads to improved performance, competitive advantages, helps you improve customer experiences and stay proactive on customer needs.

So, what kind of data do you need to start gathering and looking at in digital marketing to really make an impact? Let's dive into that next.

- Chapter 2 -

Squeezing Lemons: Navigating the Tart
Truths of Good and Bad Data

Data isn't just static numbers - surprise! When you launch a website and put Google Analytics code in your header to start tracking performance, you get numbers to work with. When you launch an ad campaign on any number of ad platforms, you get impressions, clicks and conversion numbers.

When you send an email, you get open rates, CTR numbers, and unsubscribes. Yes, a ton of numbers. But they are just that for now - numbers.

Depending on which lens you look at these numbers, you could be looking at good data or bad data. The numbers are just numbers unless you are comparing them to something in a greater context, such as a goal, industry benchmarks, or full funnel conversions.

But how do you know what you are looking at, especially if you are just taking over a new account or trying to find the best strategy to improve a campaign?

Across most funnel-related platforms, such as your website and ad platforms, you'll be able to get insightful data about your prospects and customers, including demographic data, behavioural data, engagement data, and sales performance data. Let's break these down.

Demographic data is your basic information about your users, such as age, gender, and location. Behavioural data is how users interact with your website, products and services. Engagement data includes likes, shares, comments and website clicks, focusing on how users interact with content. And sales data focuses on revenue numbers, lead conversion and other key performance indicators.

The problem is that all of these data points across your various marketing platforms, including your website, your social media, your CRM, your email list, and your paid ads could all be filled with good and bad data. Looking at the simple performance metrics may not be giving you anything useful to work with - or worse, it may be leading you down the wrong path.

In the next chapter, we'll go deep into how to calculate various performance metrics, but I want to cover good and bad data first. Why? Because I want you to think critically about the performance data you have in front of you with the filter of good vs. bad. Context is everything here.

What is good data? Good data is accurate, relevant and clean data. It's data that's not biased, misleading or simply wrong. It's also based on context.

Good data is reliable and represents the audience you are targeting. For example, if you are comparing marketing data from an event campaign targeting one of your ICPs (ideal customer profiles), it would not be reliable or accurate for your entire ICP base. Plus, since the data set is from an event, it would not be an accurate depiction of how your prospects or customers would interact with your regular content or outside of a targeted funnel. So while the data is "good" for the campaign itself, it turns into not-so-great data when applied to a different context.

In addition, data from an incorrect target audience or bad segmentation can result in unreliable data, wasted ad spend or irrelevant content that could confuse prospects and erode trust.

Here's the painstaking reality - if your data isn't clean and contextual, it's most likely useless. Here's the bitter truth about bad data; if you don't know where your data came from and you have quite a bit of it, you may be operating and making decisions based on data that's completely unreliable. And if you have these blind spots, it can lead to misguided decisions - right from simple analytics to complicated machine learning models.

How do you identify bad data? There are nine different types of data that tend to be the common denominators. While most of these live in a business' CRM, I want you to think about the number of times that you've had to copy performance data into a deck for a client presentation from Google or Facebook ads, Instagram's dashboard, etc. A single outdated or wrongly formatted metric can severely impact your data quality.

1. **Inaccurate Data**: This is data that is wrong or misleading, such as data entry errors, mistakes in data collection or faulty sensors. In marketing, an example could be that tracking is only set up on one form, but you actually have multiple forms on the website, so you are only seeing one piece of a much bigger story. This is both misleading and an error in data collection.

2. **Outdated Data**: This is data that is no longer relevant, which can be hard to determine. In fast-changing industries, this one may be difficult to work with. But the world around us can also influence when data becomes outdated. Before, during, and after

COVID, I worked at a marketing agency that specialized in fitness and gym marketing. Overnight, that entire industry was severely affected, as fitness centres shut down across Canada and the United States. When gyms could open again, one owner was confident that his core demographic was stay-at-home moms who came in for his group fitness programs during the day. That used to be his bread and butter. Now, it was younger folks, who came in to lift weights. He wasn't particularly thrilled at this new demographic, as they tended to be messy, hang out around equipment, and skip out on their bills. He pushed to get the moms back in the gym, but all campaigns fell flat. All of his previous performance and revenue data were quickly deemed outdated as moms had learned that they could get exercise and stay healthy without a gym membership.

3. **Contextual Data**: This is data from a specific period, event or campaign that is unique to a certain segment of performance. Think back to marketing performance results for an event. This marketing data can't be compared to your continuous always-on marketing campaigns, especially if you are going after specific ICPs or markets not within your usual demographic.

4. **Incomplete Data**: This refers to data that has missing values or lacks certain attributes to give you a full contextual picture. For example, think of your customers' locations. You wouldn't be able to say that you've generated a certain amount of revenue from New York if you had customers without location data in your CRM. Again, it would only tell a piece of the story, and strategically, it wouldn't make sense to draw any conclusions from this data.

5. **Duplicate Data**: Unless you have smart systems that can identify contacts based on a unique identifier, such as an email, you will most likely have an issue with duplicate data if you are on a multi-system tech stack. The same piece of data can be entered into several databases, but if not recognized or connected, it can inflate or skew the analysis and cause potential errors.

6. **Inconsistent Data**: This one comes up when a company uses different formats or units for the same type of data. It could also come up if a company isn't using the CRM fields as intended, or adding more data into fields than designed.

7. **Irrelevant Data**: This pertains to data that does not add value to the particular context or analysis at hand. And if the person looking at the data is trying to draw conclusions, it may make data processing slower

and more cumbersome - and essentially, a waste of time.

8. **Unstructured Data**: Unstructured data can be difficult to analyze if it is a manual input process. While the data itself may not be "bad" in the traditional sense, unstructured data opens up the possibility of human error, spelling mistakes, capital vs. lower case formatting issues and more. An easy one to spot could be metric units vs. Imperial units. Another one could simply be the way someone writes a date - is it month/day/year or is it day/month/year?

9. **Non-Compliant Data**: Some industries, such as healthcare and finance, can have strict data governance and regulations in place. Accessing, using, or storing non-compliant data can have some significant legal and financial repercussions, especially if used with marketing intent. Examples of regulations in place to protect individuals in these areas include PIPEDA and HIPAA.

Whether you are dealing with incorrect data or trusting a system to help make decisions for you, your data has to be validated before it can be trusted.

In Q1 of 2022, Unity Technologies experienced a significant data quality issue when their ad targeting tool, Audience Pinpoint, ingested error-filled data from a large customer. Yup, feeding a system bad data that had not been verified. The corrupted data skewed the system's ability to assess user behaviour accurately, leading to flawed advertising placements and lower campaign effectiveness - and ultimately conversions.

Overall, it's predicted that Unity Technologies suffered close to $110 million in losses due to the decisions made on bad data. The wave of bad luck continued, as investors lost confidence in the business, leading stock prices to drop and advertisers began questioning the reliability of the ad-targeting algorithms.

Shares dropped by 37% and the $110 million in question included a direct impact on revenue, costs associated with recovery, rebuilding and retraining models, and a delay in launching new revenue-driving features to help prioritize, identify and fix data quality issues.

About four years prior to the Unity Technologies scandal, Samsung found itself in the middle of a data whoopsies. In April 2018, a simple keystroke mistake caused the firm to issue 2.8 billion shares to employees in stock ownership. Samsung Securities accidentally distributed shares worth around $105 billion to employees, which was about 30 times more shares than the actual total. An employee simply entered "shares" instead of "won" into a computer and voila - 16 employees sold five million shares worth around $187 million after receiving them. The mistake wasn't caught for 37 minutes.

The costs of this simple data mistake? Stock shares dropped nearly 12%, which is about $300 million of its market value being completely wiped out in a matter of minutes. The company also lost major customers due to concerns about poor safety measures, and the company was barred by financial regulators from taking on any new clients for six months.

These are examples of how an innocent act can have a huge impact when a simple keystroke is wrong or if you trust a system to handle your data for you without any sense of quality control. According to Gartner, bad data costs organizations an average of $12.9 million annually. Shockingly, advertisers specifically waste close to 21% of their media budgets due to poor data quality, according to a 2019 study by Marketing Evolution.

It doesn't stop there, unfortunately. Research indicates that 20% to 30% of operating costs are due to bad data, leading to issues with incorrect orders and shipment delays. While it may cost you on the financial side to have bad data, it can also cost you trust in your brand and market share.

Thus far, we've covered how to start gathering large data sets and be open to the data you receive, including organizing data and validating it to ensure it's clean.

We've also now covered good data and outlined where data could potentially become bad in a larger context.

Next, we'll really narrow down on digital marketing-specific metrics to ensure that when you are looking at this data, you are doing so in a way that helps you identify scalable opportunities and ditch the data that doesn't work for your goals.

- Chapter 3 -

The Lemon Bowl of Metrics

There are two sides to marketing data and many marketers only look at one side. We'll spend some time diving into the metrics in this chapter through the lens of good and bad data, and in the next chapter, I'll explain why you need to layer in yet another massive factor - the one often ignored - and that's human psychology.

In digital marketing, every component has its own set of metrics. On a website, you have sessions, users, page views, and traffic sources. In paid media campaigns, you have impressions, clicks, cost per lead and conversions. For social media, you have views, follows, clicks, comments, and shares. In email marketing, we look at open rates, click rates, unsubscribes and bounce rates. Regardless of how you slice or dice it, there are plenty of metrics to analyze across all of your digital efforts.

While all of these metrics do tell a story in a full-funnel blueprint, there are some metrics that I want you to focus on. Those are click-through rate (CTR), conversion rates, customer acquisition cost (CAC), customer lifetime value (CLV), engagement rates, and return on investment (ROI). If you are generating leads, you could also focus on cost-per-lead (CPL).

Each of these metrics should be compared to industry benchmarks and measured against your own goals to ensure you are closing gaps in your marketing funnel and addressing issues that cause prospect frustrations. Let's break these down.

1. **Click-Through Rate (CTR)**: Your click-through rate measures the effectiveness of your ad or your email CTA. It's calculated by dividing the number of clicks by the number of impressions, which is essentially the number of eyeballs on the ad or email. You then multiply it by 100 to express it as a percentage. For example, if your ad or email received 50 clicks after being shown 1,000 times, your CTR would be 5%. Keep in mind that impressions are how often an ad is seen, whereas in email, it's related to your opens more than sends.

If you are looking at a singular ad campaign in your Google dashboard, the metrics should directly correlate to what you are targeting. But you should be cautious in using this performance data and compare it to previous ad performance reports, if you aren't measuring apples to apples - that means, exact same concept and targeting.

Where bad data could be a culprit here is if you compare your performance data and CTRs to historic CTRs and start drawing conclusions without knowing the complete context around previous campaigns. Previous campaigns could have been specifically targeted, driven to a high-converting landing page that resulted in a significant increase in CTR. External factors, such as industry changes, could also play a role in older datasets. Context is everything.

2. **Conversion Rate**: Your conversion rate is the percentage of visitors who complete a desired action, which is most likely a purchase or filling out a form. If 200 people visit your website and 10 of them make a purchase, your conversion rate is 5%. If you are looking at a conversion rate from your ad platform alone, you may be able to get a somewhat accurate conversion rate if your measuring triggers are set up correctly.

But if you are looking at it from a holistic marketing perspective, you also need to look at organic traffic and social traffic to ensure you get an accurate conversion rate. While one funnel may be working well, another may tell a different story. And depending on how your triggers for paid media are set up, you may be looking at a healthy CTR, but the website may be a hindrance for conversion, causing leads to abandon the process entirely.

3. **Customer Acquisition Cost (CAC)**: Customer Acquisition Cost is the amount you spend on marketing and sales to acquire a new customer. For example, if you spend $10,000 on marketing a month and acquire 100 new customers, your CAC would be $100 per customer.

The thing to be aware of here is that each marketing channel may be more effective than others. For example, you may be able to acquire customers at a lower cost through paid media, but do they spend less or more than customers acquired through organic traffic? It's rare that you have a singular acquisition cost for customers across all channels, simply because the strategies and tactics are so different across each marketing channel. Plus, each of them serves different purposes throughout your traditional marketing funnel.

You may find that your cost-per-lead (CPL) is lower for some lead sources than others, but that the quality of leads differs. It's important to understand what sources give you the most return on your investment and what sources play the biggest role in your revenue drivers.

4. **Customer Lifetime Value (CLV)**: Once you acquire a customer, you may be able to predict future revenue based on past data - if using clean data, of course. The lifetime value of a customer is calculated based on how much revenue a single customer will give you over their lifetime with your business.

Think about a gym; if you spend $100 on marketing and get one customer, your cost per acquisition is $100. Now, if you charge $10 per month, you will make $120 in a year, which is usually the length of a gym contract - unless it's month-to-month, in which case it is often more expensive. In this example, you have a profit of $20 on your marketing efforts. Now, your CRM may reveal that your customers tend to stay for an average of three years. You can now predict that - on average - you may make $360 from this customer. All of a sudden, that $100 isn't so bad if the return is $360. And that's just in the contract alone. That doesn't include any auxiliary services, such as personal training or added health services, such as cold plunges or post-workout shakes.

5. **Engagement Rates:** On the journey to acquisition, there are lots of little steps that are often ignored. These are called attribution points. Engagement rates are good indicators of how effective these attribution points are in your funnel.

The engagement rates are the interactions between a business and a prospect, and they're often measured in clicks, likes, shares, and comments across multiple platforms. It's important to understand how to properly measure your engagement rates and analyze how they go beyond the platform and affect behaviours in your funnel. While a platform can only capture what happens on the platform, you can get a much better contextual picture of what is going on by zooming out a bit on your data funnel.

6. **Return on Investment (ROI)**: There are three ways to look at ROI.

Siloed ROI: If you are looking at how much you've put into a single platform as part of a larger marketing effort, you're looking at siloed ROI. For example, you put $1,000 into Google ads and you got $3,000 in paying customers back. You have a return on your investment on Google. Measuring ROI this way ignores any and all other attribution touchpoints that happen in the funnel that play a role in the conversion to an acquisition.

Financial ROI: The financial ROI is the all-in return on all marketing efforts. If you put money into social strategy, website, SEO, content, email, and paid ads, you are measuring the ROI on the sum you put into marketing efforts and measuring it against your overall business profits - and potential growth. This one is harder to measure, especially if the lead attribution and new marketing efforts are not set up properly from a reporting perspective.

Insights ROI: The return on investment doesn't have to be measured in financials. While most companies add money for the sake of getting a financial return, analytical insights can also be a great ROI to learn more about what is happening in the funnels, how your varying content can affect your engagements, how your funnel is streamlined and whether there are lead gaps, and how the various points of conversions are working across the funnel. Most times, these insights provide a better understanding of how your funnels work and where to tweak, scale or revamp your efforts to lower cost per lead and cost per acquisition.

There are many additional metrics that you can track and it really depends on what your goal is. If you are trying to improve your social engagement performance, it may be worth tracking your clicks, likes, comments and shares more than your CPL and CLV.

It's important to set your goals so you know what you are measuring against. In addition, most industries have their own benchmarks for most digital marketing metrics so you can compare to see if you are close to aligning with industry standards or if you need to optimize your efforts.

All of these metrics mean one thing in an always-on campaign and quite another in a niche campaign with specific targeting and steps in the funnel. As mentioned earlier, context is everything to determine how effective your funnel is. What works in one contextual sense may not work in another.

This is true regardless of the amount of data you have, especially if it's spread across multiple funnels with multiple objectives.

Even if you have the same funnels, strong metrics to measure, and you have a good idea of your costs per lead and acquisition, engagement metrics can reveal more about your funnel attribution points.

The thing is - the funnel is never truly linear. We, as humans, do not go through a shopping experience the way it is set up to funnel us through a journey. In fact, we have many objections throughout a single sales journey and a powerful funnel has attribution points to help address as many of these objections as possible to avoid a prospect mentally checking out of the funnel.

Human experiences are not linear. They are never linear. And thus, our funnels shouldn't be linear either. Every journey is different and on average, a person needs anywhere from 3 to 50 touchpoints before moving ahead with a sale or investment, depending on how qualified and ready they are. But since we are all different, the funnels need to be flexible enough to address as many different viewpoints, objections and behaviours as possible to get as many conversions as possible.

With larger data sets, you'll be able to spot patterns and optimization opportunities that can tell the story of how people with real experiences, real feelings, and real objectives move through your lead-nurture and sales funnels.

Next, we'll dive into marketing psychology to discover how humans think - and draw conclusions - and how all of this impacts your marketing efforts and your marketing data.

- Chapter 4 -

Lemon Harvesting: Embarking on the Data Voyage

You open your laptop. You open your browser. You type the words, "best vacation spots in Italy." The search results come up and you browse through them for a few seconds, choosing to click on the one that resonates with you. The pictures look nice and they seem to capture exactly what you're looking for.

You click to book your flights, your accommodations, and select a rental car - because, sure, why not? It's all so easy and straightforward. You whip out your credit card and within 10 minutes, you've booked a summer vacation for your whole family.

Search, click, buy.

That summarizes a completely normal buying journey - right? Straight from point A to point B - no objections, no hassles, no research, and zero second thoughts about a possible better deal.

Well, sorry to burst your bubble, but this kind of buyer journey rarely happens. In fact, it's quite rare. The biggest reason for this is that we are humans. We like to ask questions. We like to challenge things. We want to be liked. We want to be understood. We want to belong.

If we are presented with a buying option and none of those feelings are met, we start to question whether this option is for us. We ask ourselves; "Is this a credible business? Who are these people? How do I know I'm not giving my money to scammers?"

Dramatic? Sure, but the trust is already eroding.

Or, there's an unclear value or relevance. We tell ourselves; "They don't seem to be for me. They don't understand my needs. It's not a fit."

Or, the buyer may not be ready - timing-wise or education-wise. So, rather than buy, they pull away. The biggest mind block we tell ourselves is, "I don't know enough yet. I need to learn more before I make my decision."

I often compare digital marketing to dating. I mean, imagine you are on a blind date and you're listening to your date talking. Review those questions again above; is this person credible? Who is this person? Am I being scammed or is this person really genuine? Do we want the same things? Is this person for me? Does this person understand my needs, or do I need to learn more?

I bet you won't be getting engaged on the first date after asking just a few questions, just like you won't invest in a service or product with just a few clicks - without asking any questions.

The point here is that customer journeys are very rarely linear. They are all over the place, jumping between social media, website, ads, emails, back to social, ads, emails, sales call, website, research…and the list goes on.

Digital marketing data - everything we covered in the last chapter, such as CTR and conversion rates - helps you tell that story. So do email open rates. Every single action tells a story.

Because the buyer journey is driven by humans, we have to layer human behaviour and psychology into every data point we examine. The concept of marketing psychology is that intersection between human behaviour, psychology and data in marketing.

And we, as humans, do not all think alike. Emotional triggers shape consumer behaviour that affects journey performance. In fact, it's not always pure logic that drives our decision-making. Biases and subconscious influences also play important roles in our decision-making. It's therefore important for marketers to understand why customers make certain decisions and help tailor the buying journey to support these decisions.

Let's throw it back to 1822. That's the year that a British psychologist named Francis Galton was born. He didn't know it at the time, but he was going to be famous for two reasons; one, he was the younger cousin of Charles Darwin - the architect behind the theory of evolution by natural selection - and two, he was going to lay the foundation for behavioural genetics.

Galton's theory was that intelligence and personality traits are largely inherited. He coined the phrase "nature vs nurture." So, one could say that he's more on the nature side - your decisions are based on your natural heritage - or, in other words, where you come from. To break that down even more - how you were raised, your values, and your belief system.

In 1878, an American psychologist entered the world. John B. Watson became known as the founder of behaviourism. Now, he strongly believed in the nurture argument. Watson argued that the environment played a huge role in perception and belief. He famously said, "Give me a dozen healthy infants... and I'll guarantee to take any one at random and train him to become any type of specialist I might select..."

Yes, classy statement. Nothing like winning over the crowd with a claim to completely control the narrative of an infant's life.

But the nurture argument is an interesting one. The decisions we make at certain stages of our lives are influenced by the context in which we are. The nurture argument can also be seen as the contextual environment in which we are at any given time, such as a stressful meeting at work. Back to Watson's claim - that he could essentially shape an infant's life trajectory; the environment would be one that Watson created for this purpose.

But what if we zoom out and look at the concept of environment differently? What if we looked at environments in our lives? How we acted as teenagers is not the same way we act as adults - well, most of the time. And how we act as kids also changed as we grew up, becoming parents ourselves. We go through shifts based on what is contextually happening in our lives and how we see ourselves in those contexts.

Have you ever walked into a store on a mission to buy a very specific thing, but ended up buying a handful of extra items? Costco, anyone? Well, one could argue that the contextual environment is incredibly powerful here. It may not be a phase in your life that's causing you to add more items to your cart - or maybe it is - but it is situational environments that influence your decision-making in the moment.

I'm going to layer in yet another psychologist to the mix here. William James, from 1842, was an American philosopher and psychologist. His theories were a bit more complex, but he believed that human experiences of emotions arise from physiological changes in response to external events. Let's break that down.

Imagine you are walking in the woods and suddenly, you see a big bear. First, your body reacts. Your heart starts beating faster, your hands might get sweaty and you may even start shaking. Pure panic starts to set in.

Then, because your body is doing those things, you start to feel scared. James developed a theory called the James-Lange theory, which basically captures this state; you feel an emotion because your body changes first.

So, for James, it's not that you're scared, so therefore your heart is beating fast. Rather, your heart is beating fast, and thus, you feel scared.

If we flip that feeling to a positive experience, such as excitement, you may feel happy. If you feel a sense of calm in your body, you may feel trust. And if you feel your heart beating in happy excitement, you may find yourself typing in your credit card details for that luxury trip to Italy, happily checking off the extra charge for first-class seats and mimosas when you board the plane.

You get the drift hopefully - your body's reaction influences how you feel.

In 1890, James published his book, "The Principles of Psychology, Volumes 1 and 2." This book has been a massive influence in my marketing career and while I would highly recommend you read it if you decide to pursue marketing, I'll just warn you now. It is just shy of 600 pages long, font size 10 and it is dry academic writing. It took me a full semester to get through. If you are up for the challenge, go for it!

If you'd prefer to skip, let me share one of the biggest takeaways from his book. James' approach to thinking isn't characterized by a straight line that follows a step-by-step process. Think about our customer journey example here; open computer, open browser, search, click, and buy.

He suggests that our thinking is more like a flowing stream that is characterized by different components of thought, including its personal nature, constant change and continuous flow. He calls this the "stream of consciousness."

He argues that our stream of thinking is ever evolving and changing. This means that our thoughts are not static or fixed, but are more in a state of flux. And he argues that our thoughts are influenced by our personal experiences and personalized interpretation of previous events. In short, our mind plays an active role in shaping our thoughts and our experiences in the world.

Imagine a straight horizontal line. The line has circles at each end. The circle to the left is our starting point - we are hungry. We know we are hungry. The circle to the right is our conclusive thought - we need to eat.

Linear path. However, it's never a linear path of thinking, according to James. Now, connect the dots using squiggly lines. Multiple lines. Each of those lines represents a fluid thought pattern. In James' example of this chart, he argues that we can all have the same thought that we are hungry and the same conclusion that we need to eat. However, how we get to the conclusion will differ. In his version, it's a language difference - one squiggly line represents German, another English, and so forth. But a line could also represent the thought process, such as "I need to eat because I'm hungry" or "I need to eat because it's lunch time." It could also be, "I need to eat because I need the energy" or "I need to eat because I just saw a picture of that chicken taco and I'm convinced."

Let's bring this back to digital marketing. You visit a website to buy a pair of shoes. You are exploring your options and you stumble upon two pairs you like. One is cheaper than the other. You may have objections to buying the cheaper pair, because you think that buying the more expensive one means better quality. That's what you were raised to believe and you've never questioned that. Or, you may be more inclined to buy the cheaper one, because it's the same materials, right? You lean one way or the other because that's how it's always been. Your inherited beliefs. Your values.

You settle on a pair based on your inherited values - Galton's theory. But do you buy the black shoes or the brown shoes? Same style, different colour. The black shoes, you argue, could go well with the upcoming event you have, but the brown ones may work best with your fall attire. Now we play into the contextual argument. In this current context, the black ones may be best for an event, whereas brown may be better long-term. Either way, the context of your environment and your needs in that moment will sway your decision-making - Watson's theory.

You go to the checkout page. You hover over the purchase button. Your heart starts racing. The price is high. You start to panic. Can you afford these shoes? Is there a better option? Will your bank call you if you click the "Buy Now" button? James' theory kicks in here.

All three decision-making theories can play a role in all decision-making in the buyer journey. And that's not all. Buyers have to be extra aware of marketing psychology tactics that are used to play into these patterns of thinking that may have them rushing into clicking "Buy Now" more often than not.

There are 15 marketing psychology tactics that I want to introduce you to in this book. You'll start to pay attention to these anytime you are presented with a potential offer to buy something, whether you're shopping online or in-store. After reviewing these, we'll explore how to read and understand the data associated with these kinds of tactics.

The first is **reciprocity**. Reciprocity is the idea that people feel obligated to return a favour. For example, if you give something to someone, they are more likely to return the favour, even if it's not a direct or immediate exchange. In marketing, it can be offering something of value upfront to a prospect and them returning the favour by purchasing something. Think of discount codes - a piece of value for the potential customer may entice them to go through with the purchase, which is the end goal.

In a B2B scenario, it could be something like an audit up front to ensure the proposal matches the exact pain-points of the company, or even a discounted rate on one service or product if other services are bought at the same time.

An indirect example of this could be a company offering to do something, such as a charitable donation or planting a tree with every purchase. This kind of reciprocity is suddenly bigger than the purchase itself and lends to a broader company or movement mission. This kind of value could potentially lead to further engagement and purchases with the brand. It's a feel-good experience - and as humans, we crave that.

The second tactic is **scarcity.** Scarcity suggests that people tend to place a higher value on something that's perceived as being rare or limited. If there's a lot of supply, the demand must be smaller. If demand is high and limited editions exist, then it suggests the product or service must be great - right!?

You'll often see this tactic being used for limited-time offers, exclusive deals, or a low-in-stock product. It's meant to create a sense of urgency, encouraging you to pull the trigger faster than you normally would and buy the product.

Xiaomi, a Chinese multinational corporation and technology company, is known for utilizing this type of "hunger marketing." The company only releases a limited number of new smartphones, creating a sense of scarcity. This leads to a rapid sellout of phones and directly creates a heightened consumer interest.

The company can then manage industry, reduce costs and build anticipation. When pushed by aggressive marketing, scarcity becomes a unique - but time-limited - sales tactic. If you are pushing a scarcity tactic in your campaign, understand that while the data may spike past industry benchmarks, it's rarely consistent in the long run. Scarcity works because it is limited, not because it's constant.

The third tactic is **social proof**. Social proof is tremendously powerful because people look for validation. They want what is correct, not necessarily the most popular. A company can tell a prospect all the reasons why their product is the best possible for them - but it is much more effective to have a happy customer share their experiences. This social validation influences behaviour, especially when there's a sliver of uncertainty.

Social proof in the form of reviews or testimonials is not only impactful to show the effectiveness and satisfaction of your business, but it also influences behaviours, building trust and credibility. And this causes others to follow suit.

Social proof is a common sales tactic on sales pages or webpages with service descriptions. For example, Airbnb leverages user reviews and testimonials to build trust with users who are looking for places to stay with positive hosts and clean accommodations.

The fourth tactic is **authority**. There's a sense of trust in companies that have been around for longer with products and services that continue to sell. Consumers are more likely to trust and follow advice from a figure or entity they perceive to have authority in a given space. Think about influencers - they can influence due to their perceived authority.

That's why brands will often collaborate with influencers who have built authority with their followers. These relationships can boost consumer confidence and trust, even for the smaller brands.

The fifth tactic is **commitment and consistency**. Once a buyer makes a commitment, especially a small one, they are more likely to stick with that commitment and act in a way that aligns with their initial decision. This can be boiled down to the simplest of actions, including getting them to sign up for a newsletter or sharing a social media post. These smaller actions can lead to larger commitments later, such as making a purchase or subscribing to a service.

This is because the smallest of actions, such as a newsletter sign-up, can open up a door for a company to build trust over time with strategic emails and slowly develop a buy-in relationship. There's also a psychological perspective here, as people are more likely to be consistent in maintaining their self-image and what they believe about themselves.

The sixth tactic is **anchoring**. Anchoring is something that happens when people latch onto the first thing they see or experience with a company. The anchoring is rooted in that people rely heavily on the first piece of information they hear, making this the anchor of the relationship. We always talk about how first impressions matter - and anchoring is a prime example of this.

An example could be showing the original price crossed out and then showing the discounted price below. The original price is the anchor, followed by the lower or discounted price. The second price is much more attractive, but the original price may set a standard as to the quality of what's being sold.

But anchoring can have a negative comparison effect, especially if the anchor - so the original price - can cause customers to focus on what they are losing rather than what they are gaining. This usually happens when the mental shift focuses on price rather than value.

The seventh tactic is **loss aversion**. The concept of loss aversion is directly related to the pain of losing something. The pain of loss is psychologically more impactful than the pleasure of gaining something, even if it is of equal value. Loss aversion is a common sales technique, where salespeople can identify everything that they will lose by not investing in a product or service. The biggest losses in this regard are time and money. Examples include listing what they stand to lose rather than gain by not completing the purchase. Knowing what's at stake can motivate consumers to act promptly.

The eighth tactic is **emotion-driven decision -making**. As humans, we have emotions. We make decisions based on our emotions and feelings. Emotional responses often drive purchasing decisions more than rational thinking. It can be everything from joy, fear and trust to pride. All kinds of emotions can drive the decision to purchase.

Marketers will often appeal to people's emotions in copywriting and images in hopes of influencing a consumer's decision to buy. Emotional copywriting and graphics can tell a story - a story that is relatable to the buyer, making them feel like they are being seen and heard.

Let's go back to Airbnb. They tap into emotions by highlighting personal stories and experiences, creating an emotional connection with potential customers. The company did this in their campaign, "Made Possible by Hosts." In this campaign, the company shared real guest stories through cinematic video ads and photography, including featuring a father and daughter who stayed at a countryside Airbnb to reconnect after losing their mom. No hard selling. Just emotions, connections, and nostalgia. The framing of the listing became that the home was a place to heal and connect, not just a place to sleep.

The ninth tactic is **framing**. This is all about how the information is presented or 'framed' to encourage decision-making. For example, framing a product as 90% fat-free is more appealing than framing it as containing 10% fat. While both statements convey the same thing, the 90% fat-free statement highlights the positive aspects and thus, can influence consumer perceptions.

Framing isn't just about a discount. It's also about how the product is framed in comparison to other products. You may have seen comparisons between products or services on sales pages. A simple comparison can put an expensive product in a valuable light if framed as being the better product compared to others on the market.

The tenth tactic is **scarcity bias**. Scarcity bias is similar to the scarcity principle but scarcity bias refers to the human tendency to place a higher value on products or services that are perceived to be limited in availability. Scarcity is the reality that something is limited, and scarcity bias is the perception that something is limited. In other words, people assign more value to products or services that they believe are limited - even if it's an artificial belief or completely irrelevant.

The eleventh tactic is the **endowment effect**. This means that people tend to value things more highly simply because they own them or they feel they are in possession of them. For example, if you were given a mug for free, you're likely to want more money to sell it than you'd be willing to pay to buy it in the first place.

The endowment effect can be seen in practical situations, such as offering free trials, sample products or temporary ownership, such as rent-to-own. These simple actions can increase the likelihood of purchase, simply because the owner starts to feel a sense of attachment or ownership of the product or service - it's a low buy-in.

The twelfth tactic is **urgency**. While scarcity is the amount of items available, urgency is more on the time factor as to how long the item is available. This is a sense of time pressure that encourages customers to act quickly. You've probably heard the ever-original statement, "limited-time only!"

Online, you'll often face countdown timers, stating "last chance" or "sale ends in 24 hours." This urgency push is meant to emphasize sales and promotions to encourage shoppers to act now and process the decision later.

The thirteenth tactic is **the halo effect**. The halo effect is a powerful one as it refers to the tendency for a single positive trait or experience to influence a person's perception of a brand. For example, if a person likes one aspect of a brand, they are more likely to view the entire brand as favourable and invest in additional services or products.

It's really about leveraging the positive attributes such as premium product quality, or attentive customer service to help expand the halo effect. A well-designed, user-friendly website can lead consumers to perceive a brand's products or services as high-quality, and thus, they may invest further in working with the brand.

The fourteenth tactic is **cognitive dissonance**. This is something you need to be aware of and try to address as best as possible by knowing your ICP (ideal customer profile) inside out. Cognitive dissonance happens when people experience discomfort due to conflicting beliefs or actions. When a person makes a purchase, they may experience doubt whether they've made the right choice.

Cognitive dissonance can be addressed by offering reassurance post-purchase through follow-up calls, emails, satisfaction guarantees, positive reviews, or even 100% money-back guarantee within a small timeframe. Offering some of these upfront in the sales process may help alleviate post-purchase dissonance, reinforcing positive consumer decisions.

The fifteenth, and last, tactic is **priming**. Priming is the psychological effect where exposure to certain stimuli influences a person's subsequent behaviour or thoughts without them realizing what is happening. In marketing, we often talk about certain trigger words that will make people feel or assume certain things. This can also be true with images, as a picture of a happy person can reinforce and prime prospects to feel more positive and confident about buying something from a company.

Even simple call-to-actions can influence priming behaviour. Basic colour theory can also be linked to priming, as colours can influence consumer moods and purchasing behaviours.

In this chapter, I've outlined quite a few factors that play into a single funnel because - well, we're human. Let's do a quick recap and tie it back to data. Firstly, a funnel is about building trust. It's not a quick one-and-done - a proposal, a sale, and happiness ever after. It's a series of events that tell a story about a perfect match between prospect and offering. In this funnel, you'll have multiple touchpoints to address some of these objections that we have as humans.

That could be in the form of social media, emails, calls from your team, interviews, presentations, and much more. How you choose to do this is completely up to you, but it does help humanize your sales and nurture experience. Now, remember Galton, Watson and James' psychological theories about how we think and draw conclusions rooted in where we come from, our contextual environment, and how we can all have the same idea and conclusion in mind but our reasonings differ.

And lastly, measuring all of that against marketing psychology tactics, such as reciprocity, scarcity, social proof, authority, commitment and consistency, anchoring, loss aversion, emotion-driven decision making, framing, scarcity bias, endowment effect, urgency, the halo effect, cognitive dissonance and priming.

Harvard Business School research shows that 95% of purchase decisions are subconscious, driven by emotion. When drawing all of this back to your analytical dashboard, my point is rather simple; marketing data does not give you the full story - just the visible patterns. Behind every click and every conversion is a human being influenced by a complex web of inherited beliefs, contextual triggers, emotional states and psychological nudges.

Reading marketing data through a psychological lens transforms it from numbers on a screen into human beliefs. Avoid looking at the vanity metrics as a measurement and instead, look for connection, resonance and relevance. It's about understanding how and why the numbers move at all.

- Chapter 5 -

Sailing Through The Lemon Waters:
Navigating the Surge, Waves...and Coping

One of the biggest takeaways from data analysis is the emergence of patterns. Patterns are only possible - and reliable - in bigger data sets. That's why you should start gathering and organizing clean data as encouraged in chapter one and keep it clean for proper analysis.

Once you start gathering large sets of data, you can start analyzing. There are three major types of data techniques I want to explore in this chapter; descriptive, predictive, and prescriptive.

These three techniques - or data buckets - can be used across all of your marketing and sales efforts, down to the simplest ad-account dashboard. It's all about what the data is telling you through symptoms and pinpoints and how human activity throughout your marketing funnel can shape your next move. To illustrate these data buckets, I've pulled on some real-life stories to help this data come to life. What I really want you to think about is how you go beyond your current thinking and analysis of your data, and how you can use critical thinking based on what you are trying to achieve with your marketing strategies.

First, let's touch on **descriptive analytics**. This is the most common method of reporting in digital marketing. Marketers will analyze last month's or quarter's performance and draw conclusions as to what could be the root cause of the numbers. Then, based on the conclusions they make, they pivot or keep going.

A huge part of descriptive analytics is understanding current trends across markets, industries, and platforms. It's also tied into insights that come out of the numbers. Remember, the numbers you see in any digital marketing platform, whether ads or social media, are indicators of human behaviour and are direct symptoms of brand positioning. For example, if an ad is performing well but conversion rates drop off on the website, that means that there's a need or interest in the ad offering, which is a great sign. But the conversion drop-off is a symptom of a deeper problem, such as trust or brand positioning.

The biggest issue with descriptive analytics is exactly this - it describes what *has happened.* And sometimes, the subtle shifts can be tough to identify when you see small decreases month over month but have a massive impact over time - sometimes detrimental.

Imagine a website seeing a steady drop of 3% traffic month over month. Over the course of a year, that's a total of a 36% decrease in traffic. That's a minor number on the monthly report, but massive if not caught early. That 3% decrease is most likely a symptom of a bigger problem that's brewing under the surface, not easily diagnosed and treated due to the slight decrease percentage.

Let's look at a practical example of descriptive analytics. A retail home furnishing company experienced a 5% decline in sales over a four-month period. In order to diagnose this issue, data analysts employed descriptive analytics to dissect past sales data by regions, product categories, store types and customer segments. This analytical review of past data allowed the analysts to identify where sales had dropped and to diagnose one or more root causes to ideally improve sales in the following quarters.

Next up, let's examine **predictive analytics**. This is when we look at past data to determine or forecast what is most likely to happen based on behaviours and trends.

Predictive models use historical trends to estimate future behaviours, including customer churn or identifying potential leads. But predictive models can also help you identify seasonal shifts and even industry shifts, especially if your ideal customers tend to shift with major industry transformations.

The great thing about predictive analytics is that you can get super granular with large data sets, including segmenting down to age groups, industries, campaign approaches, and sales. In fact, predictive models tend to be the most successful when you rely on data to get the right solutions in front of the right people - rather than analyze after the fact in a descriptive analytics model.

The Target Corporation did this extremely well when it learned how to predict a potential pregnancy in its customer base. The corporation implemented predictive analytics by examining past purchase patterns. For example, they paid attention to customers who would increasingly purchase unscented lotions and supplements. Through this data, they could predict pregnancies and send tailored promotions - without the customer ever sharing that they were expecting. This strategy was widely credited with contributing to significant revenue growth, though exact figures remain internal.

Lastly, let's look at **prescriptive analytics**. Prescriptive takes predictive analytics one step further by recommending actionable next steps based on the analysis. In other words, it doesn't just predict future outcomes but also suggests the best course of action based on data insights.

At a very high level, that could mean that the predictive analytics indicates that a particular customer segment is likely to churn due to a rising competitor. Prescriptive analytics may suggest offering a special offer to keep them for longer, while working on an improved value proposition for that segment. It's all about trying to understand what has worked in the past to address potential negatives before they materialize.

Like descriptive and predictive analytics, prescriptive analytics work best when done in segments or unique data sets. If done at a high level, you may miss some critical issues or opportunities within your customer or lead segments. It's also important to understand that the data just presents the symptoms - it's the variables in the solution that will make the impact.

Lemonade, an online insurance company, utilized prescriptive analytics through Bayesian Marketing Mix Modelling (MMM). The Bayesian Marketing Mix Model is an advanced approach to analyzing the effectiveness of marketing campaigns by incorporating past knowledge and uncertainty into a statistical model. Bayesian MMM is often preferred in situations with limited or uncertain data, as it incorporates prior knowledge and provides more flexible, probabilistic estimates than traditional models.

Lemonade analyzed marketing activities, including online advertisements and social media engagement, and compared these metrics to performance metrics for the company. Through this, the company was able to identify the contributions of each marketing channel and how each played a role in the conversion funnel. This enabled the company to optimize its marketing strategy and budget allocation to ensure continued growth and proper data-backed scaling. To no surprise, the company saw growth and improved performance.

Many digital agencies tend to rely on descriptive analytics, identifying what has worked and what hasn't in the past month or so of performance. The problem with this is that it only captures a small section of performance and hinders critical thinking and analysis, which may provide a much different picture of the performance if put in various contextual examples.

Marketers should use a combination of all three techniques to get the best understanding of the performance data, looking behind the social and ad platforms for data. While quantitative analytics is super important for the industry benchmarks and proper optimizations, it's equally as important to look beyond the dashboards to get a broader understanding of seasonality, industry shifts, trends, and public perception of the brand in question. This approach in performance data analysis will provide a more comprehensive understanding of data, leading to smarter and more data-driven decisions and strategies.

Capitalizing on all three techniques in tandem will allow you to sail through your performance reports, capturing the components of your marketing that do not work and scaling what does. In addition, you'll be able to easily navigate the waves that come in and be surfing - rather than drowning - when facing shifts or changes that are beyond your control.

Data is power - use it wisely.

- Chapter 6 -

Surfing the Lemonade Tsunami

Now that you understand what data to analyze, how marketing psychology plays a role in lead and buyer behaviours, and the different methods of data analysis, it's time to look at how people act online to capture some useful data. And what better way than to look at social media?

While social media metrics are not fantastic for predictive analytics in the full funnel, they do provide great insights into human behaviour online, and since people spend a ton of time on social platforms, it's the best place to start building brand trust.

As it stands at the time of this book, we - as human beings - spend almost three hours per day on social platforms. Video content drives the highest engagement, interactive content can see engagement rates of up to 70%. And 81% of consumers say that social media content helps build brand trust. So, while social media may not give you a direct ROI that can be counted in dollars, it can give you something many would consider priceless - brand loyalty and trust.

Social media platforms are some of the most active places to get real-time data in bucket loads. These top-of-funnel platforms are major components of any social strategy, because it's often here that trust is built, maintained and grown. Social media can be used to measure consumer sentiment and it can have a major impact on brand perception.

With every post you share on social media, you may see a constant flow of data. So many people interact with social content every day that it is a great place to gather preliminary data for how your followers, leads, and customers interact with your content.

Because there's so much content and data available, social media platforms are also great for understanding audience demographics and checking our competitor insights. You can also evaluate influencer impact and gauge brand sentiment - all things that play a role in top-of-funnel marketing. Remember scarcity, social proof, authority, loss aversion and all of the other marketing psychology tactics? Social media provides a great playground for those.

When we're talking about turning data lemons into lemonade, being consistently active on social media can give you waves of data to work with. Hence, the chapter name - surfing the tsunami. But this is where things can also get complicated for marketers. While there's a ton of data to explore, some are pure vanity metrics, while other metrics are often analyzed on the platforms alone and not in a broader contextual sense.

A major piece of the trust pie comes from social media content. A sentiment analysis plays a significant role in understanding how people feel about your brand, product, or campaign. That can include evaluating online conversations, comments, reviews, reactions to social posts; negative, positive or neutral. A negative sentiment on social could be a symptom of another issue that has surfaced in a customer-facing incident or a bad review on Google. It doesn't take much for people to speak up and the word can spread fast.

AI processing has changed the way brands can determine brand sentiment across the internet. AI utilizes data mining to determine classification and the next step for optimizing that brand sentiment. This can include gauging audience moods, identifying trends that may impact the brand sentiment positively or negatively, and suggesting data-driven decisions to enhance brand strategy. Keep in mind that while AI is helpful, it should always have human oversight for validation.

Of course, it's not only about brand sentiment. Social media strategies need to tap into all stages of the funnel, including the middle of the funnel and the bottom of the funnel. Social media is great in this regard, because the best strategies tap into genuine human needs - connection, trust, belonging and relevance.

These are psychological drivers that help with not only collecting data - they also earn meaningful engagement that can reveal deeper insights into unique audience segments, their respective motivations and values.

These analytical and qualitative insights feed into your broader marketing strategy. Understanding audience psychology and subsequent consumer action can inform and influence everything from marketing strategy to product development and customer experience.

I've pulled three examples that show social media done right when it comes to serving humans first, and selling second. All three use social media strategies to not merely count likes or follows, but also to build trust, create connections and nurture long-term relationships through authentic conversations. These combined show

how marketing psychology and smart data analysis can result in powerful top-of-funnel growth.

The first example is HubSpot and its B2B approach. HubSpot nails B2B social media by focusing on educational content that speaks directly to business owners. The content is a mix of blogs, videos, webinars and success stories that build trust by positioning them as approachable, trustworthy and helpful industry leaders.

They remove the vendor stigma and focus on community growth and partnerships through their strategic approach to content. The company will do polls and real-time Q&A to foster engagement and get real-time rich data on what their audience wants. They can then use these pinpoints to fuel targeted campaigns that convert leads into loyal customers.

This approach drives consistent lead generation and nurtures a strong brand loyalty, essentially feeding into their inbound marketing funnel. So much education happens in top-of-funnel marketing that HubSpot is able to move prospects through the sales funnel before a conversation with HubSpot has taken place, shortening the sales cycles.

Another example is Glossier and its B2C approach. Glossier, a beauty company, focuses on community and authentic customer voices. Rather than dominate their feed with their content, they encourage user-generated content (UGC) and frequently repost real customers for inclusivity. The focus on customer selling is removed and shifted to the actual people benefiting from their products. This helps build emotional trust and engagement with their core demographic which primarily falls in the Gen Z and millennial audiences.

The connection with other customers and users creates ongoing social proof and a sense of belonging, which are both powerful psychological drivers that help create powerful brand advocates. This performance data - everything from brand sentiment to engagement - helps them position products and create new offerings that are aligned with their core users.

This - in turn - helps them with customer retention and lifetime value.

The third example I want to highlight is Slack. Slack is a technology company that provides an online platform for internal and external communication. In their marketing strategy, Slack combines helpful content, customer success stories and real-world use cases tailored to various industries. Their content provides a strong balance between education and lighthearted content that helps humanize the brand.

A big part of their social media strategy is to create a community. As a result, they are quite fast in answering questions or responding to comments across all platforms. This helps build trust through reliability and shows care for users. A direct result of this is a decrease in churn and new users see the impact of the respect and dedication to the company's existing user base - it's a win-win.

Of course, the data worth extracting here is the unique type of content that gets engagement, drawing on the qualitative data that comes from the direct conversations and feedback. This, like HubSpot, provides important insights into the customer journey, the sales funnel, and improved services.

There are two major takeaways here from these examples; one is the power of focusing the marketing around human psychology and showing a direct care for customers, sales-qualified leads, and marketing leads. The second takeaway is how the data that comes from these social strategies can help you leverage useful insights that can help every stage of your sales funnel, business execution and retention strategies.

While social media can be a tsunami of content and data, your superpower lies in understanding emotions, motivations, and social behaviours on these platforms. Once you understand how to interpret the right data points, you can turn data lemons into lemonade that converts real human insights into marketing strategies that convert - and truly connect.

Of course, you're most likely not going to get it right the first time. We rarely do. Or, your initial social strategy just gets mediocre results. While time is important to get those larger datasets, testing is also important. The true power of marketing lies in optimizing your marketing efforts to scalable insights and ultimately, more revenue. This is where A/B testing becomes invaluable.

- Chapter 7 -

Squeezing Insights: Navigating the Zesty A/B Testing Terrain

Proper data analysis, where you are doing descriptive, predictive, and prescriptive in tandem, is like having a crystal ball that tells you what has happened, what might happen next, and tells you exactly what to do - without needing actual psychic powers. Less of a mess to clean up after throwing spaghetti on the wall for months.

Sure, we want to squeeze out the insights from the various data analysis techniques, but we also want to remember that we're dealing with humans, and we are complex beings. We are - truly. Ever hung out with toddlers? Teenagers? Parents? Complex.

Throw it back to James' theory for a second about how we can all have the same idea and the same conclusions but different neurological ways of getting to the conclusion; introducing A/B testing.

Since we are complex human beings, we are often different in many unique ways. And that explains how we behave and what we find valuable in a sales funnel. It's impossible for a company to develop a lead funnel that satisfies everyone who enters it and create a 100% conversion rate across the board. Even with unique personalization and segmentation, you are always going to have some top-of-funnel MQLs that won't convert while in the active post-form submission phase.

Even with the data analysis from social media, you still won't get it right. It takes optimization and testing to fully land on something that has a higher-than-average conversion rate. And that's where A/B testing shines.

A/B testing - also known as split-testing, involves comparing two versions of the same campaign to see which one performed better for a set of pre-determined criteria. You can test everything from an email, a landing page, a website, and a social post. But a word of caution here; to truly get useful data, only test one element at a time. For example, if you are testing two separate emails to see which one performs the best, don't send out two emails with two different subject lines, two differing graphic designs, and two sets of copy. If there are big variations in the test results, you won't be able to confidently say which element had the biggest impact on the results.

A/B testing allows marketers and digital strategists to make data-driven decisions without guessing what may or may not work. Assumptions and intuitions as to what will work are removed completely from the equation. You actually get the answer to what *works.* Of course, A/B testing is often done several times, highlighting different elements in different seasonalities to be prepared for future campaigns. Remember predictive analytics - looking at past data to determine what is most likely to happen in the future?

For A/B testing, predictive analytics can be extremely powerful. For example, you're A/B testing different approaches during your busiest time of the year. You are testing everything from subject lines to brand sentiment, pulling on practical approaches and emotional ones. By the end of your busy season, you should have a pretty good idea as to what worked well and what didn't. By the time the next busy season rolls around, you can use this data - alongside what is happening in the industry and seasonality - to ensure your marketing efforts pack a punch.

The most common way to do an A/B test is to compare things like subject lines, intro copy, images, and call-to-action buttons. And while those are all great things to try out, I challenge you to think broader here. You could also A/B test for humans and their unique desires. If a single CTA button got 60% and another got 40%, what does that really tell you? Is it worth it to put all of your eggs into the 60% basket? Or should you continue to mix it up?

Rather than testing one single word or phrase, focus on your ICPs (ideal customer profiles). Identify what they find valuable, what their unique pain points are, and how to speak to them. Run A/B tests on each unique ICP, focusing the direction first on the practical pain points you can help with. Make this very practical, sensible, and direct. On the second test, focus on the emotional pull. Push empathy, understanding, and provide the guidance and support they are looking for.

Once you have a clear winner here for each ICP, you can start to get granular over time with testing images, copy and CTAs. Running one A/B test by testing your subject line is not going to give you tangible results that you can use to scale. A subject line most likely won't be the asset that becomes a game changer for your efforts - it's the connection to your leads and customers - you know, the people with feelings.

It's important that you are constantly testing, gathering data to improve your experience with your prospects and customers. We - as humans - change and evolve all the time. So should your marketing. In order to be proactive rather than reactive, run A/B tests frequently.

Before you jump into any A/B testing, make sure you plan it out. There are four major steps to a successful A/B test and you should spend a good amount of time on each to get the best results possible. Once you've got these steps down, it's rinse and repeat.

The first step is to **identify your goal**. You have to set the framework for the test. Depending on what you are trying to achieve, you may need to create several A/B tests to find the most concrete results.

You can use a SMART goal framework to narrow it down. If you are unfamiliar with the SMART goal framework, it combines a **S**pecific action, a **M**easurable criterion, identifies what's required to make it **A**chievable, highlights the **R**elevancy for the cause, and provides a specific **T**imeframe.

For example, "My goal is to (specific action), which I will measure by (measurable criteria), by (timeframe) because it is (relevant to my overall objectives) and (achievable with my current resources and skills)."

Let's use email marketing as an example with the practical/empathetic approach. "My goal is to measure the impact of a practical vs empathetic approach using engagement metrics and full ROI in my emails to determine which resonates the most with my list by the end of Q2, because it is important that we speak the same language that our ICPs value. This can be achieved in-house with the help of the email team and our data analysts." It's important that you have all of the elements in a single statement and that they are specific and granular. The biggest one I often see missed? Timeline. Have a specific day or time as the end goal. Always.

Once you have a goal laid out in the SMART framework, it's time to **create your variations**. This second step is crucial as it may just lay the foundation of your success. As mentioned before, a single test most likely won't give you a firm takeaway.

The easy answer would be to tell you to test two different subject lines. But I want you to take a huge step backwards, revisit your brand buckets and your company's mission. Is there something else you can test first, such as mission-centric vs solution-centric? Once you find what resonates here, take it a step further. Does the mission-centric approach work best with leads as they're building trust with you? Does the solution-centric approach work best after you've convinced them to buy and now they just want solution-driven communications?

Or is it vice versa? Once you have A/B tested your communication style across lifecycle stages, that's when you dig into the actual email itself. Test things like subject lines, copy, images, GIFs, humorous approaches, serious approaches, practical introductions, and much more.

Just remember - only one element at a time.

The third component is the actual test itself - **running A/B tests**. When you do A/B tests, it may be tempting to run a couple of tests at the same time. Keep it stupid simple. Large data set, one test, one goal, and one analysis at a time. When running the test, keep two things in mind; use a large data set and run the test for long enough to get great results. This is particularly good with ads.

For email, consider several emails with the same test idea to get multiple results for further analysis.

The last thing to do is **analyze the results.** Now, you may be thinking that it will be easy to see a clear winner with you're results. That's often not the case, especially if you *really* know your audience. The thing is - you may get results that are closer to 60/40 than 90/10. If that's the case, keep testing. Keep digging. Keep trying. Once you find your sweet spot, you scale from there.

I'll be honest - early in my career, I was terrified of A/B testing. What if I said the wrong thing? What if I got a ton of unsubscribes? What if that single subject line just completely missed the mark? I really didn't want to step on anyone's toes. I've come to realize that this kind of thinking is completely self-serving - and I was ultimately failing my audience.

Why? It's my job to care. It's my job to get it right. It's my job to keep testing until my audience feels understood. Having the privilege to someone's inbox shouldn't be taken for granted. It's my job to earn my presence in their inbox. And the only way to earn my spot is to continue to deliver content worth reading - and not what I deem to be valuable. No, no. What they consider valuable.

A/B testing is your best friend to hone your skills, understand your audience and deliver top-quality content your audience wants to read. Let these tests be your guide for not only better results but also for better relationships. Relationships are, after all, the key to retention and long-term success.

The wonderful thing about this kind of testing is that you get some wonderful insights into your audience's perception of your brand and your understanding of their unique needs. From this, you can develop new frameworks, stronger content plans, better SOPs, and improved strategies - all from testing and analyzing human behaviour in various digital marketing channels.

Bannersnack, a company offering online ad design tools, knew they wanted to improve the user experience and increase conversions on their landing page. They started using heat maps to understand how users were navigating the page. Analyzing that information led them to create a larger, higher-contrast call-to-action button. And it made a huge difference. This is well-documented in a Hotjar case study, where Bannersnack used heat maps and session recordings to understand its conversion numbers.

Now, they had two landing page variations - one with and one without a bright CTA. The company performed multiple tests, continued to analyze both the heat maps and the conversions to understand what was happening. As it turns out, the big CTA won.

A/B tests are also used in political campaigns. During the 2007 presidential campaign, Barack Obama's team used A/B testing to optimize their website's sign-up forms and media content. The goal was to garner online attention and understand what voters wanted to see from Obama. During the election, it's all about building trust and relationships, so they wanted to capitalize on the existing interests and engagement.

The team tested four distinct buttons on the website that lead users to register for newsletters. Additionally, the team used six different accompanying images to attract users. Through various testing and combinations of assets, they were able to identify the most effective pairings that lead to increased user engagement and support. And what could be better in an election?

Now that you have a solid understanding of A/B testing and utilizing larger data sets for better performance, let's discuss some legal frameworks that come into play. Yes, just because you can easily gather data doesn't mean you're free to do whatever you want. In fact, data laws and regulations are not only in place for privacy but also to ensure that companies play by the rules. A simple mistake could cost you thousands - if not millions. Let's avoid that.

- Chapter 8 -

Sailing Through Lemon Storms with
Compliance

Now, before we start this chapter, I do want to
highlight a very important thing here. I am **not** a lawyer.
While I do work with data every day and try my best to
stay on top of as many legal changes as I possibly can in
regards to data consent, privacy, use of data, and
tracking, the advice provided in this book should be seen
as the first step of many to ensure you are fully covered.
Please do not see anything in this book as being the final
end-all be-all of data compliance and most importantly,
legal advice.

Compliance is often the boring part of marketing.
Yes, we have to follow the rules. Yes, the rules don't

always work in our favour when it comes to our strategy. But I'd rather help you set proper and good habits early on than run into some compliance storms later on. I want you to be able to have great data safeguards in place so you can sail and scale - not end up in a costly shit storm that ends up costing you everything, simply due to a data mishap.

There are two parts I want to discuss in this chapter that will have an impact on your data. At the beginning of this book, I highlighted the importance of clean and healthy data. Everything I've highlighted in this book only works if you're working with high-quality data. The second part has to do with data compliance. Let's start with quality.

Data quality issues are extremely common, which is why many companies hire a data analytics person to ensure the data is as clean and organized as possible. Every company wants to make data-driven decisions, but data input can get sloppy, human errors happen, and complacency kicks in.

If you are relying on the efforts from your team to keep the data clean, ensure they understand why it's important. Rather than telling them to input the data as part of their job or responsibilities, get their buy-in by showing them *why* it's important and *how* it impacts the business if it's not done correctly. Let them feel part of something bigger than themselves, giving them the power to help spot and address incorrect data input.

For marketers, that can include performance data in reports, time-tracking for teams, and completion of projects. But if you are leading a team, it can also be profit-and-loss reports, growth initiatives, and personal growth plans. When we set goals, they should be tracked, and data is such an honest and clear way of doing this.

Here are the steps to ensure that your data quality issues are handled and addressed. You should have a process for handling missing data, inaccuracies in the data and inconsistencies. If you are operating in a CRM with contact data, you may have incomplete data. If you are gathering data elsewhere and importing it into a CRM, you may be dealing with privacy and consent challenges. And worst of all, if your data lacks great quality, you may struggle to interpret all of the data you have, resulting in downright "noisy" data - it says a lot but nothing at all in the big picture.

The second thing to be aware of when it comes to data quality is the data-driven insights and decision-making that come out of the analysis. You want to be confident in what the data is telling you, and the strategy you put together based on the data. That's why it's important to put your data into the context of what is happening outside of your dataset, hence looking at the descriptive data, the predictive data, and the prescriptive data discussed in Chapter 5. You constantly want to challenge your data to maintain your trust in the data.

The third and last point under data quality is what is often referred to as **data hygiene**. Data hygiene is the process of "cleaning" or "cleansing" your data, deleting and removing what no longer works for you. For example, if you work in email marketing, you have worked on building your list for months or even years. It's common to see a 25% churn on lists, but these people don't always unsubscribe when they are no longer interested. They will hit spam, stop opening emails, and trash the emails. Others may change their email address over time.

It's your job to remove all of these people from your list for two reasons; they are hurting your email efforts because it's telling platforms that your content is no longer valuable (even though it most likely is) because it's looking at these unengaged contacts. And two, these unengaged contacts hurt your data. Your analytics will be skewed if you include these contacts in your open, clicks, and conversion numbers.

Let's shift our focus to data compliance. Data compliance is an increasingly important topic in North America, especially after the strict regulations coming out of Europe with the General Data Protection Regulation (GDPR). The California Consumer Privacy Act (CCPA) was enacted shortly after to ensure ethical data practices for residents in California. A handful of states are following suit.

The premise of these acts is clear. With the overflow of consumer data, laws need to be in place so consumers are not targeted inappropriately or manipulated with skewed marketing campaigns - all while protecting privacy.

It's important that you check your unique country, state, province or region's unique privacy and data regulations as the fines for violating them are hefty.

Marketers need to be mindful of these regulations. While they may possess certain data about their consumers, it's not necessarily legal for them to use it for marketing. For one, companies must obtain user consent before collecting personal data, anonymize sensitive information and be transparent about how that data is used. In Canada, that means following Canada's Anti-Spam Legislation (CASL).

For marketers, data compliance mostly falls in how you use the data you have available to make strategic decisions about segmentation, nurturing, and building consumer profiles. However, as you gather data from consumers, it's important that you protect it regardless of use case. I've found three stellar examples of what can happen when companies fail to have the proper controls in place.

Back in the spring of 2017, credit reporting agency, Equifax, faced a significant issue when it reported incorrect data scores for millions of consumers. This all occurred due to a data processing error - a data quality error. For three weeks, consumers received incorrect scores, which had a significant impact on consumers. Some scores shifted as much as 25 points - both high and low.

What's interesting is that the underlying data was correct - the scores themselves were wrong. The damage was huge. Equifax's reputation and trust were damaged. Thousands of consumers were unable to get loan approvals, faced increased insurance premiums and were offered higher interest rates.

The CEO Mark Begor acknowledged that a mistake had indeed happened in June 2022, five years later, calling it a coding issue. The company would settle with the New York Attorney General's office, which reported that about 77,000 New York residents saw scores reduced, directly affecting them. The penalty for a data quality issue score? A whopping $725,000. Plus, the company agreed to reimburse lenders and insurers who adjusted rates upwards on behalf of affected consumers.

How could this have been avoided? Equifax should have implemented a robust data validation and verification process. This internal process would help detect and correct inaccuracies before they impact consumers. Data scientists should also conduct regular audits and real-time monitoring of the systems to ensure data integrity remains in place.

Here's another example of how poor data quality can result in a massive financial penalty. From November 2014 through May 2017, Uber miscalculated driver commissions in New York City. The issue happened because Uber erroneously calculated commissions based on gross fares instead of net fares. This resulted in underpayments totalling close to $45 million across thousands of New York City drivers. It averaged out to about $900 per driver.

This meant that for about 2 1/2 years, drivers were unknowingly paying Uber's commission on the full fare, including taxes and fees that - by agreement - were the passengers' responsibility. While it is a small amount, about 2-3%, it adds up when you're dealing with over 10,000 drivers over 30 months.

As a result, Uber faced a class-action lawsuit in the summer of 2016, where drivers claimed "wage theft" and accused the company of violating its own terms of service. About a year later in 2017, the company acknowledged the mistake and announced that they were committed to refunding drivers every dollar owed - plus interest.

Regulators investigated the company and imposed settlements. Like the Equifax example, the internal process for data handling must have clear documentation and those calculation methodologies need audits and checks to ensure they run smoothly. Data handling and processing must be transparent and monitored.

The above examples had to do with data quality. However, the data you gather and use must often be accompanied by consent. If you gather and use data without the documented consent of the user, you could be in serious trouble.

And that's exactly what happened in the Facebook and Cambridge Analytica Scandal in 2016. Cambridge Analytica used data from millions of Facebook users without their consent to influence political campaigns. The company harvested personal data from up to 87 million Facebook users. This data was used for political advertising and psychological profiling during the 2016 U.S. presidential election and the Brexit referendum. Not only did this highlight significant lapses in data privacy, but also in user consent management.

Since it all started with one of those infamous Facebook quizzes, most users had no idea that their data was used for political purposes. That's issue number one - consent. Issue number two is that the data was then used as manipulative tactics, something that was later labelled as an unethical form of psychological manipulation.

The third issue was that Facebook didn't stop or prevent the misuse of data and was very slow to act after the data breach was revealed, and the fourth issue is that this data leak and misuse potentially influenced the outcomes of major democratic votes.

Needless to say, the fines were massive. For Facebook, the company got a $5 billion fine from the U.S Federal Trade Commission in 2019 for privacy violations. The U.S. Securities and Exchange Commission (SEC) also fined the social company $100 million. Lawsuits followed. As for Cambridge Analytica, the company declared bankruptcy in 2018 after legal and public pressure mounted. Key executives in the company were banned from running companies again for their unethical practices.

There are laws in place that require companies to document data consent, including where consent for data analysis and usage was gathered. In addition, transparency is required to ensure that companies are honest about what they use consumer data for.

In 2019, a lawsuit was filed after it was revealed that Apple's Siri accidentally recorded a private conversation between a doctor and a patient. It was supposedly a Siri contractor who claimed they overheard this conversation. Apple paused the program and later decided to make Siri's data collection opt-in only.

But the damage was done. There was no documented consent that the doctor and the patient had agreed to be recorded. On December 31, 2024, Apple agreed to pay $95 million settlement in a class-action lawsuit. The outcome of this settlement is still ongoing at the time of this writing, but Apple users have a right to get involved in the class-action lawsuit if they experienced any strange or unintended Siri activities between September 17, 2014 and December 31, 2024. The final hearing is scheduled for 2025.

Unlike the Facebook and Cambridge Analytica scandal where users knew that their data was shared with Facebook, Apple users had no idea that Siri had the ability to record and listen to conversations without being activated first. While the payout per user in the Apple case may be minor, this could potentially result in stricter policies and transparency changes for companies.

If you are thinking that all of these examples are only applicable to large companies, think again. Data privacy is not only a serious topic, but it is also widely recognized as a fundamental human right, particularly under international human rights law.

So, before you start stretching the imagination and get cloudy on how you use your users' data, know that you could be violating your users' fundamental human rights. That's a legal battle I would not want to get into.

- Chapter 9 -

Scaling the Lemonade Stand

Scaling a business is a common goal for many business owners and marketers are often tasked with identifying the growth levers in the data to help make that possible. What are the campaigns that performed the best in terms of ROI? What's the service that brings the strongest retention? What's happening in the market that can be capitalized on?

In this chapter, I'll briefly cover why you should use your performance data to scale your marketing efforts, how marketing psychology can play a key role in scaling, the importance of using personalization and segmentation, and building a data-driven culture among all team members. When everyone follows the data, you're setting everyone - and your scaling efforts - up for success.

First, let's discuss why you need to use your performance data to scale your marketing efforts. Your performance data gives you your key performance indicators, gives you your strongest channels in terms of full-circle ROI, and helps you identify the most common touchpoints in your marketing and sales funnels.

Keep in mind that marketing data in ad, social, and email platforms is only telling a fraction of the story. You also want to look at qualitative data that's happening in offline sales conversations and behaviour in retention emails to identify patterns and consumer behaviour that's worth capitalizing on.

Your performance data will give you quite a bit of insight into human behaviour in your funnels. For example, you may pick up behavioural triggers and buyer intent signals throughout your touchpoint content. Here's the thing - data alone doesn't drive sales. Human decisions do and these are the ones you have to find using the data. Once you've nailed what motivates behaviour, scaling is easier.

In e-commerce, some of these triggers are easier to identify. For example, cart abandonment is a straightforward signal. In B2B sales, you can look at repeat visits to the website, dwell time on certain pages, questions to the sales team and clues that signal an intent to buy.

Throughout your funnel, you can test marketing psychology principles, such as reciprocity, urgency and loss aversion to see what triggers behavioural changes in the funnel. The idea is to build funnels and campaigns that meet consumers where they are - not to convince them to move where you want them to be.

So, what moves people? As humans, we have a desire for status, and a fear of missing out - and those human psychology tricks are the second thing you need to note. So, you can layer in emotional drivers that push on these buttons. You do this with segmentations and automations that can trigger conversions and move people seamlessly through your funnels.

For example, you can use automation to segment people who repeatedly visit a landing page or a sales page and nurture them differently or escalate sales conversations. These nurture emails could have double the urgency and fear triggers to push the action towards the conversion.

When you are nurturing your prospects, it's important that the experience feels human. If it has the slightest ounce of robotics or AI, the trust will be broken.

The human sense isn't just about using "first name" in your email content. It's about the relevance of content in the sales funnel and the connection prospects feel toward your brand.

The best way to personalize this journey through any marketing and sales funnel is to use customer and prospect data, such as names, preferences, or behaviours to segment and narrow down actions. This will help you create meaningful experiences.

But you don't want to come across as creepy with an email triggering, stating that they've been tracked on a webpage. Instead, focus on empathetic messaging and a natural tone to come across as helpful and caring. You can also use social proof and familiarity to build trust.

Simple behaviour-based triggers could include emails, such as "You left something behind in your cart" or "Here's what other customers loved about this product."

While data can help you get closer to your growth goals, scaling isn't just about conversions. It's also about building a strong sense of trust with prospects and consumers. People do not connect with data and numbers - they connect with stories. And stories help build trust.

The stories that are powerful for consumers are stories that relate and connect through pain points. That's why social proof and testimonials are so powerful. They reflect the pain points of similar customers, and they put prospects and services in a different light.

It's also important to look at qualitative data and blend that into your quantitative data. For example, examine reviews, feedback, survey sentiment and more to understand the "why" behind the "what" you'll get from the clients.

Thirdly, the power of segmentation throughout the marketing funnel is critical for building long-lasting customer relationships. You want people in your funnel to feel valued, whether they are net-new prospects or customers. And while you may want to know "what" they buy for the sake of scaling, you also want to understand "why" they buy.

Why they buy is linked to your ICP personas and their unique pain-points, desires and wishes for themselves. You want to dig deep into psychographics, including motivations, values, lifestyles, fears, goals, and aspirations. While you may be able to guess some of these, using reliable data through surveys, interviews, social listening and consumer feedback to validate your predictions is great.

If you have different types of consumers in your funnel, you want to segment them even further. For example, if you are offering a health-related product, your audience segment that is healthy habit builders should be nurtured differently from your audience segment who are deemed "crisis-responders" who tend to make decisions quickly.

The more you can narrow down your unique ICPs' feelings, the better you can match them to their funnel stages. For example, one ICP may lean heavily on trust, whereas another may lean heavily on the practical outcome of your solution. How you weigh these in your funnel's content will be different each time, as some may have a heavy focus in the awareness phase, where others need more details near the conversion phase.

You can then use behavioural data, such as bounce rate, scroll depth, and click patterns to determine where those emotional disconnects happen in your campaigns so you can close the gaps and strengthen your funnel.

If you are unsure of what the data is telling you, you can always use A/B testing to determine if you're messaging is off, or if there are better - or worse - ways of communicating your message. While you want to be persuasive, you don't want to lean into the manipulation bucket. Be ethical in how you market and how you use people's data.

And lastly, let's quickly touch on overcoming data resistance. While it isn't hard to gather data, you'll always have someone in your professional circle who will choose pretty campaigns over analytical campaigns. People will often resist data-driven approaches because data is dry, unclear, or there's a loss of creative control. And while those can all be true, data - if clean and organized - doesn't lie. As you try to grow and scale with data, you should know that you may face resistance because of fear.

You need to position data as a tool for empowerment and proactivity rather than a sense of punishment, limitation or a personal dig at a creative team. Data shouldn't be the final decision maker, but should be used to drive decisions instead. Get the buy-in from the teams and have open discussions about the direction. Sometimes, you need to let people try things out and let the data tell the story to win over the team.

At the end of the day, data literacy lets everyone win. One way to frame this is to teach people that stories connect with consumers - and the data helps reveal how those stories are connecting. Data helps identify the meaning and the subsequent actions that resulted from these stories. Part of the buy-in is also updating your team when the data is clear and you can share results with them. They need to be along for the whole journey.

Here's the thing; scaling a business requires marketing data intelligence and alignment with consumer psychological insights. This will help drive sustainable growth. From the data, you can create a roadmap for your services, products and personas to scale your strategies.

Here are a couple of examples of how companies have used performance data to scale and used consumer insights and personalization to truly grow with data-driven decisions.

The first example is Yum Brands - the company that owns Taco Bell, Pizza Hut and KFC. Yum piloted an AI-powered email campaign that personalized not only who got the message, but also when, how, and what. Yum was able to do this because it analyzed past behaviour, including when recipients opened the emails, and tailored the send schedule based on past data. The company used AI to create subject lines and content blocks tailored to each person rather than a large mass email.

Using past data to improve performance resulted in a double-digit increase in consumer engagement. This resulted in more purchases and less churn from marketing communications.

Part of scaling their email efforts included AI-driven A/B testing, testing multiple email variations in real time and dynamically changing the campaigns as needed. In addition to online communications, Yum also offered mobile apps, kiosk menus, and drive-thrus.

Personalization continued here, as AI helped personalize the buyer experience across multiple channels.

If you are a coffee drinker, I'm sure you're familiar with Starbucks. Starbucks collects quite a bit of data from its customers. This happens through online accounts, rewards programs, mobile apps, and buyer behaviours. All of this information is used to personalize your experience with the company.

For example, they recommend products based on your previous purchases, give you a free drink on your birthday, and use your information to create targeted marketing campaigns. They even track the weather at the time of purchase, time of day and user location. So, if you bought a caramel macchiato on a Tuesday because it was raining, don't be surprised if you get emails or ads served up around this time when it's raining.

Like any company, Starbucks also segments by behaviour. They analyze who buys what, when, and why - which means they aim for longevity, frequency and preference data. They also track behaviour in emails, so if you haven't engaged in their emails or visited a store in a while, they may send you a personalized offer. This is all driven by predictive analytics to try to capitalize on you coming in to re-engage with Starbucks.

But this kind of data-driven decision-making doesn't just work on splurge purchases, such as food and coffee.

It also works on larger purchases. Honda used data to personalize the car-shopping experience. After customers secured financing for a new Honda vehicle, Honda Financial Services (HFS) sent each buyer a personalized video walking them through their specific finance plan. The details included everything from the monthly payment amount, payment schedule and total term. The video also included the buyer's name, vehicle model, and payment terms.

The psychological component here was that Honda made the customer feel valued and appreciated, rather than a transaction. The personalized walkthrough reduced anxiety and confusion for new buyers, and it built trust with Honda, while empowering customers with clarity. There were no surprises, and it resulted in a reliable and trustworthy one-on-one interaction.

The results were outstanding. There was a higher engagement, as customers continued to watch the videos to understand their respective agreements. In addition, by having this clear communication in video format, there were fewer calls in regard to payment clarification. Lastly, the personalization tactic resulted in a retention boost, as people felt seen and informed. This increased the likelihood of them staying with Honda Financial Services.

At the beginning of the book, I briefly highlighted Netflix as an example of how powerful data-driven decisions can be for personalization. So, it only makes sense to go back to that example here. Just like Yum, Starbucks, and Honda, Netflix also collects and analyzes a ton of consumer data. In fact, original content gets approved based on historical data for similar genres and completion rates. For example, "House of Cards" and "Stranger Things" were confidently green-lighted based on data insights.

Netflix uses machine learning to analyze viewing habits, such as likes, watch time, and abandonment to identify taste communities and anticipate interests. You may also have noticed that artwork for shows and movies changes over time - all geared towards increasing engagement.

As for encouraging a data-driven culture, Netflix treats the conclusions drawn from the data as hypotheses to test, not opinions to broadcast to the public. The company uses science-centric experimentation, such as A/B tests at scale, and continuously validates UX and content to capitalize on choices and engagement. All of these data-driven changes resulted in improved customer satisfaction and business growth.

So, where do you start? Remember the form logic idea from Chapter 1? Well, getting your prospects to share details in the forms when they submit gives you some information about them as ICPs that can help you create a personalized funnel experience that addresses some of these painpoints and streamlines a roadmap for them - completely automated.

Just try it out and let the data guide you.

- Chapter 10 -
Squeezing Psychology into Every Drop

Hopefully, by now, you've realized that trying to identify a direct ROI on a marketing campaign is layered. Marketing isn't just about clicks and conversions. It's also about building trust in a crowded market, challenging the industry through consumer-driven data, and most importantly - people.

Whenever you see a metric for an abandoned cart, an open rate, or a single click, remember that it is a human brain that's making the decision. While I've covered quite a bit in this book about data across your marketing efforts, this final chapter will highlight how everything comes to life in a marketing funnel. I'll cover how psychological principles play a role in every stage of the marketing and sales funnel. That's because humans are part of every stage, and we're emotional, intuitive and social. And data will give you the insights you need to make better decisions.

Just like squeezing a lemon yields concentrated flavour, extracting psychological insights from every stage of your funnel will sharpen your campaigns, making them more effective. We'll go through four different funnel stages; awareness, consideration, conversion, and loyalty/retention.

At the top of the funnel, we have the awareness stage. This stage of marketing is all about capturing the attention of the market and building trust with net-new consumers and staying top of mind for existing customers. Even if a customer hasn't purchased or been in touch in a while, clever brand awareness campaigns can reignite the desire to re-engage.

The goal in this stage is to spark interest and emotional intrigue. Psychology gives you the framework to do this effectively, and remember, the digital metrics will reveal the effectiveness of your approach.

In this phase, it's important to keep it simple but impactful and memorable. It's about cognitive ease as the brain prefers simplicity. Use clear copy, recognizable visuals and minimal distractions. When someone looks at your ad for three seconds, they should be fully able to understand it clearly without mental hurdles or puzzles. The less effort it takes to understand the ad, the more likely it is to be remembered.

You also want to tap into emotional triggers to build trust. Leverage emotional connections, such as curiosity, joy, or even fear to stand out. You want people to stop and think for a second - and feel understood.

While social proof is important here, you don't want a full testimonial to take up your brand awareness campaign. But you can use subtle hints, such as "trusted by 10,000 happy customers" to show social proof. People follow the crowd, and there's a fear-of-missing-out element when talking about a group of people or using scarcity triggers. No one wants to be left behind.

There are fun ways you can do this. For example, think about Coca-Cola's "Share a Coke" campaigns. It was simple, it was personalized with people's names on the cans, and it created emotional triggers of both understanding and inclusivity. It became a movement that carried the social proof along with it. It turned an ordinary product into a viral social movement.

To achieve success for an awareness campaign, you have to satisfy three criteria. One, you want to increase brand recognition and make your audience aware of your brand, product, or message. Two, you want to generate interest and engagement to spark curiosity and emotional resonance. And three, you want to reach new and relevant audiences to expand into untapped demographics.

As prospects move down to the consideration phase of the marketing funnel, the goals shift. In this stage of the marketing funnel, it's all about educating prospects by providing deeper insights into products, services or the brand. You also want to build trust and credibility, use social proof, and show that your business produces reliable results. Lastly, it's all about encouraging engagement and exploration, such as taking specific - and measured - actions.

Multiple channels contribute to the consideration phase - and they can often work together. I've chosen to highlight branding, social media, and email marketing to help show how psychological concepts play a role in each of these.

When it comes to branding, it's important to build familiarity, as this is a huge component of trust. Keep your visuals, tone and message aligned. Trust and feelings all tie into the emotional resonance. If you understand your audience, you should have a good understanding of what emotions will drive action. Tap into feelings, such as a sense of adventure, comfort or belonging, and use branding to evoke these feelings.

Psychology also plays into the perception of value. In those initial brand awareness phases, psychological pricing techniques can influence how customers perceive the value of your brand and services. If you want to stand out amongst your competitors, establishing yourself using strategic positioning is a powerful move.

One move that really brings people close to a brand is the feeling of being understood. Nostalgia can help do that, as nostalgia helps create emotional bonds by associating your brand with positive memories and experiences. John Lewis' Christmas ads from the United Kingdom are renowned for the emotions they bring out. These ads often tell heartwarming stories that resonate with viewers, which helps strengthen brand perception and drive sales during the holiday season.

On social media, you need to create a balance between visuals and influence. On these platforms, we - as humans - have very little patience. We scroll super fast on our devices and we only stop when something catches our eye. In fact, marketers only have a few seconds to make an impact.

Visual psychology can influence a scroll stop. Colours have a tremendous impact and each colour represents something different. Blue builds trust, yellow signals energy and green represents growth. Visual hierarchy also helps guide attention, including guiding people to take action.

Storytelling and social proof always win on social media, so sharing user-generated content, reposting customers' success stories, and influencer endorsements tend to tap into the herd mentality. Everyone wants to follow the herd, so this is a great way to show a community surrounding and supporting your brand.

And when someone is chasing to fit in, the fear of missing out (FOMO) can quickly be another psychological tactic that can convert. The fear of missing out on whatever the herd can provide is real - and consumers will often convert rather than be left behind.

We see this in fashion all the time. Fashion brands use influencers to activate trust and consumers want to replicate what the trusted figure wears and uses. They want to feel included and part of the trend rather than left behind. Not only can influencers rally the masses, but they can also help establish trust and social proof with endorsement alone.

When it comes to email marketing, you have the option to personalize the communication through segmentation and dynamic content. Personalization, beyond your typical first-name merge tags, can help increase trust and engagement. You want offers and sales pitches to be sent to a list as specific as possible to increase the chances of conversion. Reciprocity is great in email marketing, because the more value you provide in email, the more prospects build relationships with you. And in the spirit of reciprocity, they'll feel compelled to give back - often in the way of sales.

If you fall into the e-commerce bucket, use urgency for sales or deals to push time sensitivity. Plus, tracking people's past purchases can help you predict what they want to buy next based on similar consumer behaviour. This can help both with segmentation and personalization, which will highlight relevance and convenience.

In the conversion stage of the market funnel, it's all about turning that interest into action. The top goals of a conversion campaign are to drive immediate high-intent action, such as purchase, signing up, or making a booking, and to remove any barriers that may surface in the decision-making process. And lastly, you want to maximize ROI from all warm leads, capitalizing on the interest built in the awareness and consideration phases of the funnel.

There are a couple of marketing psychology tactics you can use here, especially if trust is built. Subtle nudges can reduce friction and increase conversions. Anchoring bias, for example, can help if you present a higher price first, followed by a mid-tier option. This positioning can cause a higher conversion rate in the mid-tier offering.

If people are dropping off at this stage in the funnel, you could try offering a small action, such as a free trial or a tool. If this ends up providing an ROI - financially, mentally or emotionally - they are more likely to follow through with a larger purchase or investment.

Of course, how the offer is presented also matters. Framing your copy to be 90% fat-free is more appealing than 10% fat. The benefit has to outweigh the downside. It's better to focus on the wins rather than the losses.

All of the smaller actions that you do to include prospects in your brand community add up. These prospects are more likely to remain consistent and take larger actions down the line. In marketing, we often refer to these prospects as Marketing Qualified Leads (MQLs), as they require more "marketing content" to convert. This is where social media, email and even paid ads can continue to provide touch points in the funnel to build trust and move them closer to a conversion.

In the loyalty and retention stage of the market funnel, it's all about increasing the customer lifetime value. Here, you want to encourage repeat purchases, cross-sells and upsells. You also want to use loyalty programs, provide personalized recommendations and provide exclusive offers to keep customers engaged.

You do this by strengthening your brand affinity and emotional connection with your customers and clients. You already won them over during the sales process, so it's about continuing that momentum by reinforcing trust throughout consistent value adds, great service, and authentic communication. If customers feel seen, appreciated, and part of a community, they become fans and will advocate for your business.

And once you have advocates, you'll get referrals, reviews, and inspire user-generated content. There are a couple of marketing psychology tricks to keep in mind in the loyalty and retention phase of the cycle. This is a phase of the market funnel that serves two purposes.

The first is keeping the customers happy so they become repeat buyers, extending your lifetime value. The second is that they can push to be advocates for your business, pushing net new leads into your awareness phase - with some pre-built trust already due to your loyal customers.

The goal in the loyalty and retention stage is to build long-term relationships built on value. Retention is all about reinforcing the psychological connections you've already built throughout your funnel, including the endowment effect, consistency, emotional memory and reciprocity. The more you can make it feel like a relationship rather than a business transaction, the better the outcome.

The endowment effect is all about how when people own or experience something, the more they value it. Your funnel shouldn't just be about converting them to a sale - making them feel like a transaction. They must *experience* your brand, your customer service, and the value you bring to show them they are a valued piece of your business.

This should be the core of your retention strategy. Provide value and make them experience what your business is all about - and create a consistency plan. This will not only build trust as a thought-leader path but also reinforce the trust that they had during the conversion phase.

We often talk about branding as not being about logos, colours and designs. Other misconceptions about branding are that branding is the same as marketing, and that only big companies need to invest in branding. Branding is all about how you make people feel. It's a strategic asset that shapes perceptions, guides buyer decisions, and compounds over time.

When we discuss this in the loyalty/retention phase, it all comes down to branding. People remember how you made them feel throughout the marketing and sales funnel, as well as after the sale. As part of the loyalty phase, did you give some special attention to bigger clients? Did you provide early access to a new service before offering it to the masses? Did you offer specialized webinars to continue building relationships with customers? Did you keep them up to speed on industry changes that could have an impact on their business and the service they have invested in with you?

You can use value and education to continue to nurture relationships to increase the lifetime value of the financial relationship. It's all about having their back and making them feel better and be more prepared about their roles in their unique situations - whether it's work or life.

There is a little warning here. It's all about education and persuasion. Steer clear of tapping into manipulation. If a person feels manipulated, it could ruin your entire reputation. You could spend years building your business reputation and brand, only for one person to completely destroy it overnight.

While you want to use psychological marketing tactics to build trust, you want to steer clear of a few as well. For example, avoid dark patterns, such as hidden opt-outs in email marketing or corporate communications, as they can erode trust and backfire. Plus, it is illegal. In addition, always explain the "why" behind actions and requests. This transparency helps people feel comfortable complying with your requests. If you just tell them to do something without a reason, they may feel uncertain or become confrontational.

Plus, your customers are smart. People can usually tell when they are being manipulated. Focus on clarity, kindness, and real connection.

Here's the thing about marketing psychology - you are tapping into people's subconscious. It is a powerful tool, so it's important to use it ethically. If you start pushing the boundaries and manipulate through fear, pressure tactics or false promises, it could be detrimental.

You'll often hear that good business practices are all about prioritizing your customers. And while a business wants to generate sales, they also have to earn the sale. And they do this through trust, transparency and building relationships with clients.

Nike once came under scrutiny for poor marketing communications. Nike ran an advertisement on X, formerly known as Twitter. The ad was created by an affiliate, The Sole Supplier. It showed a photo of shoes with the copy, "Now just £26 at Nike!" However, the advertisement did not indicate that this offer was limited to children's sizes 3-6 in the UK.

This was deemed to be misleading and false advertising. Regulators labelled this as a bait-and-switch pricing, which included a headline bargain which drew clicks and engagements, only to be told that the offer didn't match the ad. The other lesson here was that Nike was held responsible for affiliate ads run on behalf of the company, even though their business affiliate partner, The Sole Supplier, had written the copy for the ad.

The ads were banned by the UK Advertising Standards Authority (ASA) in September 2024 and Nike - along with all business affiliates - were told to ensure future ads clearly disclosed pricing and sizing.

Transparency upfront needs to be as prominent as the call-to-action. So yes, marketing psychology can be your superpower but only if you use it wisely and with respect to consumers.

Marketing isn't a sales pitch - it's a conversation with the subconscious. Data helps us understand what works, but psychology helps us understand *why* it works. Great marketing doesn't just track the numbers. It also tracks behaviours, emotions, and trust, which is ultimately part of the ROI.

- Conclusion -

When you first cut open a lemon, it's unpredictable. Will it be juicy or dry? Will it be packed with seeds, or be ready to squeeze? All you really know about the lemon is that it has potential - the potential to be more than just a lemon.

Marketing data is the same. At first glance, it's chaotic - full of seeds, pulp and contradictions. It's just a bunch of data points of all shapes, sizes - and issues. But when you start applying pressure, you start extracting something meaningful - something you can turn into something better. Just like lemons into lemonade.

That's what this journey has been all about. Not just squeezing numbers for the sake of reporting, but pressing into the *why* behind the what. In your marketing metrics, whether on social media, paid ads or email, you'll find the human truths as to what is happening in your efforts. It's all about moving beyond the dashboards and understanding the business in a broader context.

In this book, you've learned how to read and understand data differently. You've learned how to sift through the noise, challenge assumptions about data, and see how data without context is flat. Psychology helps give it dimension, which helps drive a bigger ROI beyond the financial ROI.

Now, your questions should be "what does the data say?" and "what will I do with it?" Because great marketers aren't collectors of numbers and metrics. They are meaning makers, pattern finders, and trust builders. They are great storytellers in a broader context than just the data dashboard.

Hopefully, you've taken a few lessons away from this book. I'll quickly go through some of my favourites from each chapter.

First, let go of perfection. You don't need to know everything to start. Just start collecting data and develop a clean and consistent framework. Avoid early assumptions and let the patterns shine through over time.

Second, understand and remember that not all data is created equal. Always question the source, the method and the motive. You cannot compare apples to oranges in your analysis. Garbage in is garbage out, so don't be afraid to lay down the hammer and get better data to work with.

Third, only measure what matters. In digital marketing, you often have to sift through many vanity metrics that don't mean much in a marketing context. Plus, metrics are meaningless without context. Always-on campaigns vs funnel-specific metrics require different analytical lenses. KPIs must always align with actual business outcomes, not just activities.

Fourth, always remember that behind every click is a human. And the human brain is shaped by emotions, bias and behaviours. Incorporate psychology to decode what can't be explained by data alone. And remember that trust and connections are built over time - just like any other human relationship we have.

Fifth, don't be scared to go beyond the platforms. Use descriptive, predictive and prescriptive analytics to see what your platforms aren't telling you. Analytics can surface unseen behaviours and hidden signals.

Sixth, while top-of-funnel brand awareness is often ignored in a marketing funnel because of the difficulties of measuring direct ROI, it's actually a goldmine. It's foundational to build relationships with empathy, rather than aggression further down the funnel. Every single touchpoint is a chance to show you understand your audience.

Seventh, always test your hypothesis rather than assume. A/B testing reveals truths you can't always guess your way to. Don't start with simple subject line testing. Go beyond that and use A/B testing to test changing shifts in your ICPs to fully understand how your audience changes over time. Optimization is ongoing, not a one-and-done.

Eighth, respect the rules. Data quality, privacy and compliance aren't just checkboxes. They are trust builders. Responsible data practices are marketing advantages in disguise.

Ninth, scale with substance. Growth without connection is short-lived. Scale with psychology - not just with budget. Personalization, segmentation and a data-driven culture are your secret weapons to success.

And lastly, squeeze psychology into every drop. Marketing funnels don't work fully unless you understand how humans make decisions. Each stage - awareness, consideration, conversion, and retention - requires a tailored psychological lens. The best marketing respects the human behind the click.

Better marketing isn't investing in new tools. It's better thinking. So my question to you is: how will you squeeze your next drop of data?

"The most powerful force in marketing isn't data. It's understanding."

- Malene Jorgensen

www.ingramcontent.com/pod-product-compliance
Lightning Source LLC
Chambersburg PA
CBHW071600200326
41519CB00021BB/6819